Transact

Transform

Transcend

Becoming a Thoughtful Leader: Stories from the Journey

Kenneth E. Russell, PhD

John Ruppel

Transact Transform Transcend
Becoming a Thoughtful Leader: Stories from the Journey

Edited by Becky Scott & Christian Russell

Cover photo by: Kenneth E. Russell, PhD *Old Southport-Supply Road, Mosquito Branch, North Carolina*

Illustrations by Ella Johnson

DEDICATIONS

Ken

A few years ago, I began my academic research on the topic of the *leader effect* that occurs when new leaders are brought into organizations. Working alongside of and learning about leaders has been informative and exciting, with lots and lots of stories to share! We hope you enjoy our vignettes! In addition to my family and friends, John and I are pleased to dedicate this book to YOU!

ex nihilo legatum fit

John

This book is dedicated to YOU, the person reading this book . . . for you to have the 2Cs (Courage and Commitment) to look into that mirror and awaken to your inner self looking back at you. To empower your inner self to lead your life from a position of confident love, joy, and a reverence for life from the epicenter of your heart — the core of your very being. To have faith, confidence, and conviction in yourself as you lead. To be resolute as you help to empower and inspire others to follow your leadership example. To help awaken others to realize the true leader within themselves, to be the best leader they can be. Know that the decisions you make today as a leader, shape the world for all of us tomorrow.

CONTENTS

FOREWORD

Kate Lewis

When I first met Ken Russell three years ago at a local IT association event I was organizing, I was fascinated by the questions he asked and his curiosity. I grew to know Ken and his accomplished career, and how he serves the academic community bringing technology and people together as a Chief Information & Innovation Officer. Knowing Ken's focus on continuous education and interest in transformational leadership, I introduced him to one of my good friends, John Ruppel, who was teaching a course on DevOps Leadership for DASA (DevOps Agile Skills Association). John and I had known each other for over a decade and he had become an expert and thought leader in the DevOps Agile Leadership and Coaching space as the US Ambassador for DASA over the past five years. John and Ken had instant chemistry, and they both went on to become the first certified trainers in North America to teach and certify future coach instructors. A few months ago, when John and Ken told me that they were writing a book together on thoughtful leadership, I was excited to be one of their first readers. Then I had the honor and privilege to be asked to write this foreword for their book.

Leadership is a complex and multifaceted topic that has been studied and discussed for decades. However, in recent years, there has been a significant shift in how we practice leadership, from a transactional approach that focuses on results, supervision, rewards, or punishments—to a more modern leadership style with an empathetic and thoughtful approach that values relationships and emotions. In this book, they will explore the evolution of leadership theory and practice, and how it reflects the changing needs and expectations of our society. This book will examine the challenges and opportunities that leaders face with the current workforce, and how they can develop the skills and mindsets that are essential for effective thoughtful leadership.

As someone who is focused on continuous learning and growth in my leadership skills and abilities, I find this book on transcendent leadership to be a MUST read for all executives and future leaders. In a world where we are trying to evolve our organizations and cultures to be great places to work, where employees are proud and happy to be a part of our companies, it is imperative that we as leaders find new ways to engage and retain talent. As leaders, we set the tone for the culture and organization, and need to find ways to embrace a multi-generational workforce that has evolving needs and priorities. We need to create a safe workplace for diverse teams where sharing new ideas and feedback is constructive and people feel like their opinions are heard and valued. This book discusses how leadership can evolve from transactional to transformational (where most people are trying to be) to the future of transcendent and thoughtful leadership (a new concept introduced by John and Ken).

As the founder of Connections Consulting Partners, I am focused on the future of work, and helping people discover their passions and values and build fulfilling careers. I find this book to bring a new innovative perspective to leadership. John and Ken explore how we as leaders need to utilize a high level of empathy and Emotional Intelligence (EQ) to promote a safe organization where learning curiosity and mistakes are embraced. Showcasing how a transcendent leader should be comfortable listening, asking questions, and seeking input. Where this new leadership style embraces vulnerability and humility and does not mean that the leader has to be the smartest person in the room or the person with all the answers.

This book is the recipe for how to take your leadership skills to the next level of self-awareness to meet the higher-level needs of your team, to increase productivity and retention, and to grow high-performing successful teams. Every leader wants to upgrade their team's performance, production, and satisfaction—and this book introduces new concepts on how to achieve these goals.

I have admired the work of John and Ken's careers separately over the years, but this book is a demonstration of their collective intelligence and how bringing two innovative thought leaders together can result in some truly futuristic concepts. They share a passion for helping empower people to become their best while adding value to their teams and organizations. This book is the perfect blend of John's work on self-actualization and personal improvement, and Ken's work on organizational change management and leadership development.

This book is intended for anyone interested in learning more about leadership, whether you are an aspiring leader or a tenured leader. We hope that this book will inspire you to reflect on your own leadership style / potential and to embrace the power of empathy and thoughtfulness in your personal and professional life. This book will help you uplevel your skills as an executive leading your team and organization to new levels of success. It all starts with you.

Kate Lewis
Founder
Connections Consulting Partners

FOREWORD

Christine Aykac

First I met with John, who introduced Ken to our group! It was *symbiotic*—our group of like-minded folks. We discussed the leadership, team developments, and organizational issues. We had a great time discussing our experiences and challenges in leadership. Gradually, our discussions led to more fruitful ideas and insights about leadership.

As we delved deeper into our discussions, it became evident that there is an art to thoughtful leadership. It is not just about having a title or position of authority, but rather, it is about being able to guide and inspire others towards a common goal effectively. While I concentrated more on skills development and adaptive leadership, John and Ken concentrated on thoughtful leadership as a skill that can be learned and developed through experience, mentorship, and self-reflection.

They discussed leadership as not just about directing others but also about creating a vision and motivating others to work towards that vision. They believed that a thoughtful leader considers the needs and perspectives of their team members and finds a way to align them with the overall goal. This book is a result of their hard work.

I present this foreword with great anticipation and genuine excitement, for it is a contemplative journey into the landscape of leadership through the insightful pages penned by Ken and John. As remarkable beacons in the field of transformational leadership, their combined wisdom and experience illuminate a path that transcends traditional models and encapsulates the essence of adaptive excellence.

This book is a testament to our evolutionary potential as leaders. It underscores the need for understanding individual growth and advocates an enlightened approach to leadership—one that is mindful of the dynamic complexities of human interactions and organizations.

Thoughtful leadership, a principle that reverberates throughout their teachings, isn't merely a concept but a profound turning point the authors experienced firsthand. It underscores the significance of adaptability, showcasing how a leader's flexibility in style can ignite significant change and progression in their organization. With the skills, proficiency, and fortitude to discern, choose, and participate, a thoughtful leader is always engaged and present, never retreating to an outside perspective. By embodying these qualities, a thoughtful leader creates a constructive and positive environment that supports the growth and success of the entire organization.

This shift from *transactional* to *transformational* to *transcendent* leadership is beautifully illustrated by their adoption of the mnemonic "**LEAD**" (Listen, Empathize, Absorb, Discern). These four pillars stand as guideposts, not only shaping their principles but also serving as an invaluable framework to those who aspire to make a heartfelt impact within their circles of influence.

Ken and John's leadership taxonomy—identifying and delineating between transactional, transformational, and transcendent leadership—provides readers with a revelatory framework. The book discusses the characteristics and limitations of a transactional leader, the inspirational nature of a transformational leader, and the aspirational vision of the transcendent leader who seeks to rise above for the collective good.

Within these pages, the authors assert that well-rehearsed routines and rigorously mapped strategies are only part of the equation. They believe that the true alchemy of leadership is achieved by nurturing a robust belief system within oneself and cultivating an environment where every team member can grow, evolve—and ultimately thrive—in the light of shared values and collective goals.

Furthermore, the book delves into poignant personal anecdotes that echo the principles of transformational leadership. Through stories, readers will uncover tangible proof that when leaders embrace adaptability, they can catalyze a culture of innovation and resilience within their teams.

As you leaf through this book, allow the shared wisdom to resonate within you. Embrace the insights to bolster your journey to becoming a more effective, compassionate, and visionary leader. With inspiration and education entwined in its narrative and a personal touch that speaks directly to the heart of aspiring leaders, this book is set to reignite a passion for excellence and transform your understanding of what it truly means to lead.

In essence, this is not just a book about becoming more than just a leader; it's an eloquent roadmap guiding you toward becoming a beacon of thoughtful leadership.

To the leaders of today and tomorrow—may your journey be transformative.

Christine Aykac
Learning Strategist & Adaptive Leadership Coach
Wareness Training & Coaching

PREFACE

"Leadership is hard to define and good leadership even harder. But if you can get people to follow you to the ends of the earth, you are a great leader."
~ *Indra Nooyi*

Navigating the path to becoming a better, more thoughtful, leader requires an understanding and awareness of how individuals grow and evolve, how everyday transactions can morph into significant transformations, and how mindset, intent, and an informed heartfelt approach can drive organization value.

This book examines the activities, capabilities, and experiences of three types of leaders: *transactional, transformational,* and *transcendent* (as well as the transitions between each) to help navigate and clarify a path toward becoming a more *thoughtful leader.* Leadership knowledge, skills, values, and a strong belief system enable and equip an individual, but more is required to rise *above the fray* and become the leader required for a given moment or situation.

What is *thoughtful leadership*? At their core, a thoughtful leader is a *listener* —not just with their ears, but with their heart, their experiences, and with an *informed gut.* The thoughtful leader also routinely *empathizes* with their team—taking the time to lean in and share experiences, pay attention to the epidata swirling around everyone, and being aware of what is going on within the organization. Being a sponge and *absorbing* and synthesizing activities and happenings is a hallmark of a thoughtful leader, as is having the skills, proficiency, and fortitude to comprehend the whole environment of their organization—*discerning*, participating, and not retreating.

What may be most surprising—when you get to the root cause, the bottom of the need, the heart of the issue, etc. of being a leader—everything boils down to the *thoughtfulness* of the person looking back at you in your mirror. We'll come back to this person—yourself, or more specifically—YOUR self, throughout this book. This is on purpose, of course, because stripped of all excuses and distractions, what is left is ... YOU! Or, more pointedly, thoughtfulness emerges from deep within you (your *self*).

CHAPTER ONE

Introducing Transcendence

"If your actions create a legacy that inspires others to dream more, learn more, do more and become more, then you are an excellent leader."

~ Dolly Parton

An initial question might be—*what makes a leader?*

It's a valid question. And the answer can be wide-ranging. A leader can simply be the person in charge—a role filled by fiat for reasons unknown—or even by default, not based on skill, seniority, aptitude, or experience.

Other questions emerge as well. What is there to be led? Is it a process? A team? Managing task-driven activities is an inherent part of being a leader. Such tasks can be simple or complex, recurring or one-time, and even time-boxed / interim in nature. Teams can be ad-hoc and temporary or long-standing with social, historical, and cultural implications and expectations.

Better questions may be: How can I become a *better leader* regardless of how I got to the position? How can I recognize various types of leaders and apply that knowledge to discern my own leader style?

Finally, how (and when) can I *transition* from one type of leader to another—and should I?

"Trans" is a compelling prefix used quite a bit in our language. It comes from Latin and simply refers to movement from one to another. When we say transitioning, for example, we are moving *across* from one thing to another.

As an example, and to introduce the use of *vignettes* in this book, following is a quick call out—*a story*—to help illustrate the concepts, practices, and processes described in a way that may be more meaningful and memorable.

Vignette

The Propinquity of You

I met my new team in the usual way, that is—via email introductions. We were scattered across the globe, working for a large Silicon Valley-based tech company. "Hello, nice to meet you. Tell me about yourself." So, we began … disconnected but immediately productive, efficient, and effective. We were cleaved together because of our individual experiences and skills, but only tacitly— this was a reorganization after all, common in large corporations and driven mostly to balance teams, sate specious span-of-control whims, or merely because previous reorgs hadn't achieved desired outcomes. I was assigned as leader, but the company's expectations were likely driven by my success as a proficient manager of measures and accompanying metrics, not because I was expected to be inspiring. They probably weren't as concerned as to *how* I accomplished what I did, just that things got done! We set about to complete our tasks and assignments—merely *transactional*.

Within a few weeks we were able to meet in person at our first offsite meeting at the company headquarters. Finally! A chance to *connect*, have *conversations*, and *collaborate*.

Slipping into a transformational leader role, a role where the leader *listens* more than they talk, observing and sharing more than they declare, I asked about expectations, aspirations, and ideas for our team. I received polite and perfunctory responses—"I want to be a team player," "I want to do the best at my job," and "I want for us to succeed in the eyes of the business." All well and good, but that makes for more of a *transactional* team, doesn't it? What makes a *transformational* team? How can a transformational leader make a difference?

Transformational leaders endeavor to get teams to share (and not hoard) their ideas and thoughts but it's challenging because building trusted relationships is difficult and takes time. My approach was simply to give the team ample opportunity to start talking with one another. An amazing thing happened: once they began to feel comfortable their guards started to come down, their anxieties began to abate, and collaboration ensued!

Laughter invaded the room and we started to coalesce as a team. A transformational leader provides the space for such collisions to occur. These *ah-ha moments of discovery* occur when you are in propinquitous situations—*nearness*. Nearness works well in person, or via a hybrid environment. It works well in a digital environment. The goal is to provide the *space* and the *time* for people to convey and relate their stories about themselves. A transformational leader enables these *collisions of experiences.*

Where things become transcendent is a bit more subtle. A *transcendent* leader leverages all the skills and attributes of transactional and transformational leaders and is at once all of these things. But in addition to the tasks to complete, assignments to fill, trust relationships to build, and stories to share, a transcendent leader stays *above the fray*. Simply, this type of leader works to maintain a perspective that enables observation, attention, and consideration of events and activities swirling about the team that tend to go unobserved and unconsidered — the things that tend to be missed and ignored.

A transcendent leader pays attention to the details. I picked up on the fact that two of my new team members were fluent in Portuguese. I pulled them aside during one of our morning breaks and asked them to start conversing in Portuguese when we returned. I suggested it could be about anything, the weather, things they did last night — but to keep the conversation going even after everyone reassembled. It was interesting to observe everyone as they returned and settled down, yet suddenly drawn in and absorbed into the "foreign" conversation going on. Because I asked them to continue past the expected end of the break period, others in the room felt uneasy — this was not normal, not convention.

The brain works well during such times of *chaos* and *disorienting dilemmas*. It was unexpected, but in that moment, they were disoriented and that's the key for the transcendent leader — the brain learns best when it is challenged and when it is disoriented. A *transcendent* leader takes the time to consider all the tools, talents, and resources available and leverages them in new and different ways — *above the fray* —

things that aren't part of the toolset of the typical transactional or transformational leader but rely more on a leader's ability to be *human* and *aware*. —**KER**

Lessons can be learned from making the unfamiliar familiar, and storytelling is a great way to help transition a concept, idea, or thought from theory to real-world. Refer to these stories / vignettes throughout this book as helpful tools—offering perspectives, experiences, insight, and wisdom. Look to them as examples of where leadership models developed, emerged, and (perhaps) changed or transformed.

The most enduring indicator as to whether an individual is an effective leader is the extent to which they are perceived as such by members of the organization and other stakeholders. Regardless of leader type or style, a resilient leader is able to *transition* as appropriate and necessary— flexible, practical, and able to be the leader required by the organization.

This book will endeavor to describe the possibilities of transitioning across three types of leaders: the *transactional,* the *transforming,* and the *transcendent.* Effective leaders are combinations of all three, and all leverage attributes needed for a given situation at one time or another.

CHAPTER TWO

A Thoughtful Leader's Journey

"The secret of change is to focus all of your energy not on fighting the old but on building the new."

~ Socrates

---

*V*ignette

Wisdom from the Surf Shack

I was in Long Beach, CA, at 7am sitting in a rustic seaside

---

shack, having a breakfast burrito and orange juice. As I gazed out over the ocean watching the local surfers paddle out for the next set of swells, Ted chuckled and said, *"You can always enjoy the view, but the food is even better."*

Looking at Ted, my Dad's best friend, you would not believe who, and more importantly what, he was. Ted was one of our nation's leading and world renowned (true) rocket scientists. He led the creation of many of the US's spacecraft. My Dad, Ted, and their school buddy Glen, who built rocket engines, would get together in Cape Canaveral where they would watch Glen's rocket engines propel Ted's rockets into space.

Over our breakfast, I looked Ted in the eyes and asked, *"What does it take?"* I wanted to know what I needed to do to be able to lead programs, teams, projects—just like him. He stared back without blinking and after a long pause, he noticed I was serious.

Ted sized me up and asked me this double question: 1) "Do you believe in the golden rule of treating others as you would like to be treated and that you can abide by the golden rule regardless of what is going on?" 2) "Do you believe you will have the strength and courage to talk to and present the reality of the situation, regardless of what is going on?"

I pondered this for a moment and responded with a resounding "Heck yeah, that's all it takes?" With my outburst, Ted choked on his breakfast burrito, lost his balance on the stool he was sitting on, and burst into uncontrollable laughter.

From that weekend on, half of my time with Ted and his family was learning leadership through his eyes. Some of the other half was helping Ted with his flower beds. One of Ted's hobbies was horticulture and I consider him an expert at floriculture. No one nurtured and grew flowers as amazing as Ted.

As you are reading, you may be wondering what this has to do with your leadership journey. *Everything*. This book outlines a blueprint for what it is and how to grow as a leader and succeed at the three levels of leadership. Your journey is personal, which only you can manifest via YOUR experimenting, failing, listening, learning, absorbing, mentoring, coaching, teaching, and collaborating with others along the way.

Ted's two questions were my foundation and basis of how to build the strongest and most credible TRUST possible in the quickest amount of time. Maintaining balance in life and the lives of those around you is the truest path to *bond* and build *trust*. You demonstrate that by living life equal to the work, task, or job at hand.

Many years later, at the end of our last breakfast together at the surf shack, I asked Ted for additional pointers or guidance. He motioned out to the surfers and said,

"Leadership is like surfing, you have to FEEL the wave." There are all types of waves—and your teammates, tools, and methods are your board. Trust them and lean into the wave together with all you've got. Don't lose sight of how and what you are—be humble, have confidence, be fair, and firm. Most importantly, don't forget to have some fun while you are at it. You only get to ride that particular wave once! —**JER**

A journey begins with a first step and for the thoughtful leader, that first step is often coming to an understanding about what type of leader you are (or are planning to become). Circumstances can impact a leader's journey, and as with any journey, obstacles must be dealt with, managed, or removed.

The table below provides an overview / framework of a typical leader's journey. The evolution of a thoughtful leader starts with being *transactional,* focused on tasks and delivery. The next phase is *transformational,* where leaders work to build collaborative teams, ideating and colliding, and building trusted relationships. Finally, a *transcendent* leader endeavors to stay *above the fray*—that is, they pay attention to the things that often get missed (details regarding team members, external influences, competing priorities) and are always *listening, empathizing, absorbing,* and *discerning.*

Transactional Leader	Transforming Leader	Transcendent Leader
Sets Direction	Amplifies Direction	Discerns Direction
Aligns People and Processes	Optimizes Resources and Processes by considering consumption and creation	Listens and becomes aware of Organizational Value (Resource Tuning)
Motivates & Inspires	Promotes Collisions to enable discovery	Empathizes and Absorbs .
Produces change by creating and maintaining order	Transforms an organization by optimizing the value of shared knowledge	Nurtures an organization by leaning in to interpret, shape, and evolve
Always Aware (Situational Awareness)	Anticipates potential outcomes and experiences	Awakened to opportunities, imagination, and the possibilities of *what if*
Superpower: Clear, direct, and consistent communication	Superpower: Transparency through vision connections, conversations, collaborations, commitments, community	Superpower: Ability to discern (spider sense)

Transactional

- Sets Direction
- Aligns People and Processes
- Motivates and Inspires
- Produces change by creating and maintaining order
- Always Aware (Situational Awareness)

Transforming

- Amplifies Direction
- Optimizes Resources and Processes by considering consumption and creation
- Promotes Collisions to enable discovery
- Transforms an organization by optimizing the value of shared knowledge
- Anticipates potential outcomes and experiences

Transcendent

- Discerns Direction
- Listens and becomes aware of Organizational Value (Resource Tuning)
- Empathizes and Absorbs
- Nurtures an organization by leaning to interpret, shape, and evolve
- Awakened to opportunities, imagination, and the possibilities of what if

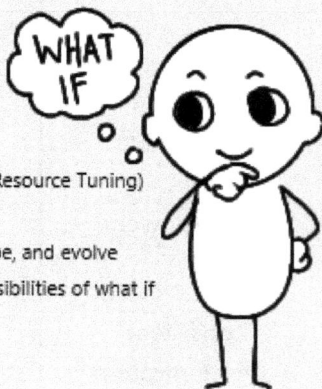

The ability to grow, transition between thoughtful leadership styles, and evolve is directly dependent upon:

- The ability to forgo one's pride, ego, what a person thinks they know, and being *open* — meaning opening one's mind to new possibilities, perspectives, and sources of information

- Capable of *feeling* and *believing* in these newfound possibilities, perspectives, and sources of information

- Courage & Commitment (2Cs), responsibility, accountability, and a willingness to bring new possibilities and perspectives into existence

This framework for growing, evolving, and transitioning into a *thoughtful leader* can be used as a general guide for recognizing elemental characteristics but it also helps with understanding the value of becoming the right leader for a particular situation. All three types detailed here encourage a *belief in oneself*, (their inner self — what some may call the soul). An example would be the leader *senses* there may be an issue, breakdown, or stress within the team that will impact their ability to achieve a result. A *belief in others* is paramount as well — many minds and hearts coupled and networked together are better, will outperform, and will lead better than a single individual on their own.

The above foundation of bringing together openness, ability to feel information, and becoming resolute in one's beliefs clears the pathway and enables a leader to think beyond typical or popular methods of leadership. To represent, participate, and evolve along with the three types of leaders highlighted here, a leader will have to listen to what their intuition (their informed gut) is telling them in real time as they are experiencing a situation.

The value in the thoughtful leader's journey is in navigating and getting the most out of each leadership experience — recognizing that challenges, trials, and tribulations are an opportunity to test the leader, and the results (although sometimes painful) are *evolution* and *growth*.

Small Chunk or Micro-Leadership Mindset

A catalyst for leaders transitioning between phases of leadership is the need to be more dynamic. Leaders must be able to react and respond in a real-time manner, within the timeframe a situation demands. Leveraging a *micro-leadership mindset* (where a leader provides guidance, direction, and mentoring with *focused points* of instruction / learning) enables a leader to become more *experiential* with the organization. This direct and *deep-dive participation* addresses specific areas of need, keeps up with complexities, disruption, and the evolving requirements.

Leading by using a micro-leadership mindset develops and improves the ability to lead iteratively and dynamically in real time. With experience, leaders *self-realize* and determine their personal evolution and growth. A leader's acquisition of leadership skills builds and expands via experiences (time in the seat—both successes and failures) and enables more challenging leadership opportunities with greater variety.

The value-add from this approach is the growth of confidence within the leader. Growth comes from the opportunity of increased experimentation which is enhanced through granular and very specific leadership opportunities. The greater the number of iterations (experiences), the more inclined the leader is to get out of their comfort zone and take risks. The result of the leader being exposed to a greater variety of experiential learning and (leading) opportunities is the confidence to take on new, even more challenging, leadership opportunities.

V*ignette*

Micro-Leadership in Action = Results

It was day one of a new opportunity, being the leader of a Data Center. The interview process had spanned over a month, meeting with executive stakeholders, team leads, and lead engineers. What I found interesting was that during all the interviews, there was always an executive sponsor present. Now that we were beyond the interview process and finally to my first day, it was time to have a team meeting with the team leads and engineers — without the executive sponsor present.

I opened the meeting by asking: "What is going on?" There was a long awkward silence and then one of the engineers spoke up: "We aren't speaking up right now because we don't know if we can trust you."

For the next hour, the team and I had our first real, honest in-person conversation regarding what was going on and getting to know one another. After the conversation, I thanked the team for trusting in me and asked to regroup the following day. During the conversations up until the following day's meeting, I was continuously making notes, breaking down the leadership needs into their smallest or most granular leadership opportunities, what I termed "15 minutes of leadership".

The following day, I started off the team meeting by asking

about their Big Hairy Audacious Goal (BHAG). BHAG, from Collins & Porras (1994), is where you define a goal with the intent to intrigue, challenge, and compel people, inspiring the team to act. Once the BHAG is defined and agreed upon, you lead team members in having them publicly and openly commit their agreement to take on this goal and next steps.

From a micro-leadership mindset, BHAG was the first leadership opportunity which I used to get the team aligned and to agree on a single common goal. After 15 minutes, the team agreed that the number one priority was to improve their quality of life, which could be accomplished by changing the working environment from being reactive to proactive. For the next few hours, the team and I broke down what and how the team would change to become proactive. When we were done there were about 25 topics, tasks, and chunks which equated to or required *15 minutes of leadership* like what I had done with BHAG. I then asked the team who would be the best leader for each and we all assigned and shared the responsibility of leadership amongst the team.

In the weeks and months ahead, the team using this micro-leadership mindset combined with a networked leadership model created a transformational culture based on the value and belief that everyone is a leader who could lead by vision and transparency. Regardless if you were the leader for the backup routine for the day, the leader for the implementation of a new storage array, or leading the overall data center operations, we would break down the real-world leadership challenge in front of us into its granular leadership opportunities, prioritize, and start executing accordingly in real time. —JER

As outlined above, today's leaders must be dynamic, present in the moment, respond in real time, and have a method to handle the rate of change for real world situations at hand. Observing the most successful leaders over the past decade, a common pattern to their approach is evident—they leverage the micro-leadership approach.

Unique Paths

A thoughtful leader's journey and path is defined by each leader. Everyone's journey and path are different because each person is different—their life experience is different, and their life's purpose is different.

Vignette

Tear it Down, Then Rebuild

I remember my first time helping to lead my organization's adoption of Agile. A few months in I remember putting my head in my hands, wondering what I got myself into. Well, it was my first version of what I call the "experiential journey". In real-time, I was solving challenges and coming up with solutions by deconstructing or unraveling my past. I found myself becoming open to new ideas or interpretations of leadership and, more importantly, what leadership could be. This helped me break leadership elements into their simplest pieces, so I could put them back together in a way that best fit my iterative way of working. Then I could create a new leadership persona with a focus on leading in a manner which was right for me, my team, and that particular situation.

I realized the true lesson being learned, the value of taking an experiential micro-leadership approach, was the ability to *empower* myself and my teammates.

I realized that I was truly in charge, responsible and accountable to myself for my own leadership evolution... *I own it*. No one can do this for me, no one can take this away from me, no one controls my reaction to what is provided to me, being done to me, going on around me, being pushed onto me, or being fed to me.

One of the most valuable realizations of taking an experiential micro-leadership approach is that *there is a unique path—what works for me and my team.* As I like to say: do *what works for you and yours.*

As I break down the information provided to me into its granular leadership elements, I can select what I need and use—when needed—and decide *when* and *whether* to move forward on my leadership journey at my own pace. —**JER**

With the world speeding up, as people's lives become busy, and people find themselves being pulled in many directions, there originates an opportunity. The opportunity is to try out different ways of leading and to experiment with different techniques, methods, or approaches with what is going on right now around the leader.

Empowering Others

Helping other leaders emerge, particularly the next generation of leaders (paying it forward, providing experiential learning opportunities, or engaging a team in a succession planning exercises) is a critical responsibility for the thoughtful leader.

What better way to achieve these results than to empower others? Understanding the magnitude of challenges a leader may face, a leader has to *know* and *believe* they are empowered. What better way to believe than to feel from deep within yourself?

Ambiguity, change, and (yes) even *fear* seem to fill our lives with a constant churn. Remember to take a moment to consider the value (or values) that have been significant on your journey to becoming … well, you!

- What would you say *drives / motivates* you?

- Was there a *fork in the road moment* in your life?

- Did you have a mentor pass on *words of wisdom?*

We become accustomed to dealing with problems, challenges, and opportunities (tested?) along the thoughtful leader's journey. More than a few of us would say *that's what makes us leaders!*

Transact Transform Transcend

CHAPTER THREE

Awareness

"A leader takes people where they want to go. A great leader takes people where they don't necessarily want to go, but ought to be."
~ Rosalynn Carter

Vignette

Rock You Like a Hurricane

The windshield wipers were doing a poor job (in my opinion) as they tried to keep up with the hurricane-force winds, rain, and waves. It was not unusual to see the blue or

---

green water of the wave as it broke upon the windows of the ship's bridge and then see the wave crash down amidships onto the deck shattering what it hit. The thunderous "WHOOOUUUMPPPHHHH" would send a series of shockwaves and reverberations throughout the ship, strong enough to knock your glass or plate off the table. Almost all of us on the ship were praying that the welders who built that ship had done a good job.

Why were we here? Our starboard (right) amidships winch and traction system for our underwater tethered vehicle had broken while diving with 3,000 meters of tether overboard. With the storm's fast approach, the only option we had was to secure the winch and wait out the storm at sea. Basically, our multi-million dollar research vehicle was now a boat anchor at the end of a long line, swinging in the depths of the ocean's water column. We were in 7000 meters of water, but the storm energy, winds, and currents were taking us off course towards the coast where there was shallow water. Since the vehicle was hanging off of the starboard side, the only direction we could turn the ship was right. If for any reason the ship had gone sideways into those massive waves, chances are I would not be sharing this story.

On the bridge we had over two centuries' worth of experience from the world's leading quality ship captain, first mate, ocean explorers, scientists from various backgrounds, US Navy Officers, and Specialists of various disciplines such as myself. We had one focus, and that was to balance this ship, in this storm's energy with the vehicle hanging over the side, with limited steering and speed capabilities so that we could maintain a very slight forward headway going straight. Our ability to maintain that balance of life and death, mission success or failure, was simply our AWARENESS.

Any twitch or change in the storm's dynamics like wind direction, wind speed, wind gusts, wave height, ship systems operating flawlessly, sea conditions, bottom depth, ocean debris, currents at all depths of the water column in the ocean, the winch system maintaining its traction and the vehicle being secured…etc., collectively, we ALL had to be AWARE and be able to respond correctly within seconds.

As a deep-sea navigator being trained by the world's elite in ocean navigation, GPS (Global Positioning System) technologies, underwater transponder nets, sonar, and so much more, this by far was one of the greatest challenges I have faced. This experience is where I learned first-hand what it means and what it takes to be AWARE. Most importantly, I learned what it means to be successful at AWARENESS. —JER

Awareness—*being aware*—is one of the foundational capabilities enabling a leader to be tuned in to what is going on inside of themselves, within their team / organization, and throughout the environment and world around them.

Using a submarine analogy, awareness is the *sonar which enables the submarine to conduct its operations, succeed in its mission, and bring the crew back to port safely.* As a leader, your awareness enables you to operate in the best way for the situation (situational awareness), position you and your team to achieve the greatest amount of success for that particular situation, and work in a manner which is best for all those concerned.

As you grow and ascend in your leadership skills and abilities, so too will your awareness skills evolve. Your sphere of awareness will expand, creating new capabilities and a heightened sense of awareness. Below is an excerpt of the thoughtful leader summary table, where we have pulled out the row depicting the evolution of awareness.

Transactional Leader	Transforming Leader	Transcendent Leader
Always Aware (Situational Awareness)	Anticipates potential outcomes and experiences	Awakened to opportunities, imagination, and the possibilities of *what if*

How do we apply our awareness to our current leadership position? The leadership theories of Warren Bennis and Burt Nanus (1985) introduced by the U.S. Army War College and used to describe today's world is a great start. They introduced us to the acronym **VUCA** (Volatile, Uncertain, Complex, Ambiguous). We have added in another C, (Conflictive) to represent as **VUCCA** (Volatile, Uncertain, Complex, Conflictive, Ambiguous).

Today's leaders find themselves in unprecedented times. Leaders have never had to deal with the volume (amount) and frequency (rate) of VUCCA elements being present at the same time, increasing and compounding their impact. More leaders and their organizations are coming to the realization that traditional ways of thinking and doing are not working anymore—some would say they're collapsing.

Understanding how to evolve as a leader— observing, evaluating, and analyzing—requires a hard look at what goes on within the organizations around us. A common thread can be found within *organizational awareness*.

Organization Architecture & Awareness

Organizational (or Organization) Awareness is the practice of helping organizations discover, optimize, and mature their ever-evolving work environments. Organization

Awareness assesses an organization's *tolerance for change, ability to absorb new information,* and *history* in an effort to determine the overall readiness for change. It addresses the *structure of an organization,* its *governance, culture, politics,* and *espoused vs. in place* processes.

In an on-site, physical, or in-person working environment one of the more common ways to gain organizational awareness is to conduct some variation of a *walkabout* or *Gemba walk.* The term Gemba walk comes from Taiichi Ohno and Norman Bodek (1988), an executive at Toyota. The objective is to observe workers and their teams working in their normal environment and have conversations about the workers' ideas for what is working well, what is not, and share ideas for improvement while gaining insight and understanding of the people.

Often overlooked is an organization's *history.* As a leader evolving the organization, it would be advantageous to understand if something was previously introduced, discussed, decisions made, attempted, or not attempted in the past. For example, introducing an idea that had been attempted before—and failed—would likely carry *organizational baggage* that must be mitigated before giving it another try. An idea may be a good idea, but gaining buy-in will require knowledge and

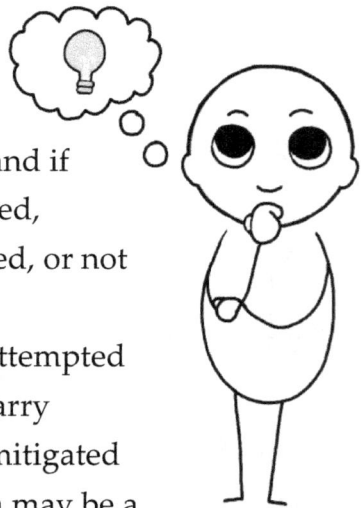

fallout (including both *technical* and *cultural* debt) from its history.

Most Agile, DevOps Adoptions, and Digital Transformations fail due to an organization's culture. Culture is one of the biggest factors—yet one of the most glossed over—impacting an organization. The thoughtful leader is aware and follows a robust transformation sequence (leveraged by DASA, and others): *culture, mindset, people, data, process* (the flow), and (finally) *tools*. Being aware of culture and the subsequent required elements is fundamental for success.

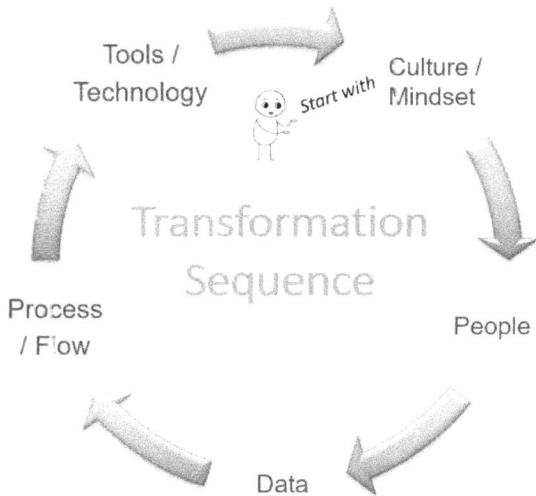

Tools / Technology

Culture / Mindset

Start with

Transformation Sequence

Process / Flow

People

Data

Another important element to be aware of is the "tolerance for change." Specifically, how willing to change is an organization? Have they been successful in the past? Have their transformation efforts really been change efforts? On a scale of one (1) to ten (10), with one (1) being absolutely no change is desired to ten (10) where change is celebrated, what rating would you give your organization, culture, leaders, and people?

Knowing and understanding the tolerance for change is often overlooked during the evaluation and planning stages—not being realized until there is resistance to a change effort. By then, it is often too late for quick corrections and a hard stop / pause may be necessary to mitigate things before attempting to move forward. This is often referred to as the difference between what is *espoused* (what is said or believed to be factual) and what is *real* (what is factual). Typically manifested in a cycle of change that may be better called a cycle of *what the heck* change because it recurs so often in organizations.

Having awareness of the surroundings and environment, as well as an organization's history, culture, and tolerance for change provides a solid foundation for the thoughtful leader. Growing or expanding awareness helps distinguish the winners and losers: those organizations that embrace and accelerate their journey—and *those that hesitate.*

CHAPTER FOUR

Environment, Framework, and Community

"There are two ways of being creative. One can sing and dance. Or one can create an environment in which singers and dancers flourish."

~ Warren Bennis

Vignette

Environmental Necessities!

Creating an environment that promotes creative ideas and encourages leadership to develop from *within* is critical. An organization prepared with a robust framework for success

---

builds a community where there was once perhaps a smattering of talent, ideas, and concepts. Much like the role of *impresario*, a thoughtful leader creates, assembles, and yes, often finances the environmental necessities for a thoughtful organization.

Clarity is an important attribute for a leader. A great line from Warren Bennis (1991) blends it with another great skill, *effectiveness*: *"When I was most effective, it was because I knew what I wanted. When I was ineffective, it was because I was unclear about it."*

I feel the same way—when my day is cluttered with routine, it's difficult to do what I call *real* work. I often tell my children to avoid spending too much time trying to be *normal* in life. Instead, they should endeavor to be *extraordinary*. For me, trying to be *normal* has never gotten me past the status quo. Only when I'm being me (ready and open to being creative) do I seem to make a difference. This is the type of environment I try to seek out or create. —**KER**

Establishing an effective baseline for an environment and community to flourish is key for the thoughtful leader. Equipped with an effective (even simple) framework of *guiding tenets*, thoughtful leaders can make a big difference—quickly. They can make bold moves and do the *extraordinary* when only *normal* was expected.

Consider the following guiding tenet transitions:

From	To
Transactions with vendors	Collaborations with partners
Careening	Strategic
Organizational clutter	Maintaining the machine
Chaos, ambiguity, and fear	Recognizing and responding to the role *change fatigue* plays in a rapidly changing environment and community

Any one of these guiding tenets can help signal and communicate the transition from something normal, to something extraordinary. Consider the mindset changes for an organization culture that routinely *careens* vs. one that becomes more *strategic*. Imagine the shift in attitudes merely by changing the way the organizations refer to and cultivate their outside resources: would you rather rely on a *vendor* when there is an emergency, or a *partner*?

Vignette

Meet the Congress

Imagine my surprise when I walked in on the first day of work for a large US corporation as the head of a group of architects. I walked into a *Congress* of architects. The word Congress should concern you. Ordinarily, you make a *team* or you make a *group*. Or even a *cohort*. But a Congress?

That was the first indication that something was very, very wrong. When we talk about the *Peter Principle*—about people being elevated to positions beyond their capabilities or training—it's often in the sense of someone just made a mistake, or someone didn't care, or someone wasn't thinking. However, in some organizations when traditional methods of promotion are not available (such as salary increases or additional benefits), managers and leaders will tend to offer titles instead. This is what happened to the title of *architect* at this large corporation, which had, at that time, been loosely defined. The title was available and offered for almost any promotion in lieu of an *actual* promotion.

So imagine my surprise when I was introduced to the *copier architect*. Or the *project manager architect*. Or even the "make something up here architect".

Be careful of organization structure. It matters—it matters a lot. And once you assign a title or position to someone, it's very difficult to take it back (or to fix the problem). —**KER**

Vignette

No Surprises in the Lineup

One of the most important lessons learned in the beginning of my career as a leader was the first time I had to fire a team that I had nurtured, grown, and evolved. This team was operating far above expectations, achieving a level of success no one thought possible. Out of an entire team only one resource was going to remain. At lunch time I called a team meeting with everyone but the person who was to remain, shared with them that this team was being let go, and provided insights into the conversation and demands from the owner. There was a really long, awkward, and powerfully emotional silence. I broke the silence myself by walking to each individual, looking them in the eye, shaking their hand or giving them a hug, and thanking them for their amazing support, effort, and achievement. For the next hour, the team gathered their belongings and went out the door. However, I felt letting the team go was not the correct decision or right path forward.

One of the major lessons learned for me was the suddenness or surprise which resulted in a shock effect on the team. They had risen to such heights and then out of nowhere, WHAM, they were hit with joblessness. I then vowed to myself I would never be placed in the same position again, that I would be transparent and true with people, and always ensure everyone knew where we stood with each other, our customers, and the business.

About a year later I was reading Jack Welch's book *Jack Straight from The Gut* and this quote jumped out at me "If I learned anything about making this (firing someone) easier, it's seeing to it that no one should ever be surprised when they are asked to leave." (p.44) When I read this I realized that this was the answer I had been searching for and what I needed to adopt as my philosophy when I had to let people go. —**JER**

Being Bold

Vignette

Boldly Forging Ahead

It was 10pm at night when my phone rang. My friend was calling—he was being asked to join the leadership team for a cyber security startup. The call was short and to the point. My friend explained the situation, his excitement, and his trepidation.

My response was "be *bold*"!

Be bold. What? How? He was out of sorts. We agreed to pick this up the next day.

The following day I reached out to a senior sales executive, and they joined in on the conversation to help and support the cause. For the next two days, there was a flurry of ideation, brainstorming, mentoring, and most important of all, helping my friend become *comfortable* with the *uncomfortable* (and realizing when and how to be bold).

Being bold is simply confidence wrapped up in *preparedness* and a bit of *faith*.

We all worked together to create a vision for his new cyber

technology opportunity that would demonstrate his agility, skill, and confidence for the role. Here is a version of what we came up with:

- *Take time to understand the business* —how data, process, tools, and technology impact the business

- *Clearly communicate* and work to *motivate* the team—make the vision a reality

- *Learn and value the talent* on the team and how they can be *brought together* to create desired outcomes

- *Translate previous successes* to new opportunities

About a week later, I received a call from my friend. He was in! He was on his way to starting the next chapter in his (leadership) life all because he took a leap of faith with his skills, empowered by being bold. Most importantly, my friend now understood what it FELT like to be bold. —JER

A thoughtful leader must be **BOLD**:

Broad

- Understands the business
- Understands technology and how it impacts the business

Open

- Motivating and creative
- Leverages the power of communication

Loyal

- Taps into the specific talent of the organization
- Recognizes the value of differing perspectives

Deep

- Is credible
- Can walk the talk

As an example, consider the shift required to morph a *culture of "no"* to a *culture of "let's discuss"*. A **bold** leader understands such a transition will take time but is open and creative about how to get to the result. The **bold** leader knows where the right resources and talent are because they have *not yielded to evaporation* in their role and have remained credible to the team, and able to *walk the talk.*

Data

Vignette

Data Manure

While helping to build a large research facility, my boss turned to me and said, *"Make sure we can do something with this data, I don't want it sitting around here like so much manure!"* And, with that a model was born!

The research facility was very large—petabytes of genomic data, researchers and scientists with IT folks following them around, and the best technology on the planet. With so much *data*, my boss was concerned (rightly so) that there'd be a danger of it never turning into usable *information.* **—KER**

Data—and how we *manage data*—has always evolved. Long before we had the zeros and ones of binary code, we had synapses firing in our brains from observations and experiences. Life is data! We are surrounded by data. In fact, the rallying cry of many data scientists has been *Data Are Screaming (and it's time for us to listen!).* But, listen to what, exactly? Data without context, without *management* are of limited value. Data must become, at minimum, information configured and arranged in some meaningful way. The leader in the story above was right, but likening data to manure—it's quite an image! How we produce and collect data is important, but how we ensure those data evolve into something more ... is the goal!

Insight & Wisdom

Vignette

Sunlight on Data

Nothing quite like sunlight on data to change them into *information* and *knowledge* ... then on to more meaningful *insight* and *wisdom*. The source of the sunlight may change over time, but don't let your data sit in the dark. Expose it to light and put it to work! —**KER**

Are there things out of the control within the organization impacting how things get done? These impacts may be *positive* or *negative*—have a small impact, or something larger, more profound, affecting the ability to flow value to the customer. The more *insight* into the surroundings and the environment, the more opportunities are revealed to make an improvement, reduce risk, or exposure.

The thoughtful leader leverages insight and experiences to develop *wisdom*—inspiring and informing creative solutions, working with novel resources—inside or outside of the organization (including with customers), and cultivating an ability to tell the good from the bad. Within the last few years, the dynamic role of technology has morphed our hunger—and our *expectations of our data.*

Data — Information — Knowledge — Insight — Wisdom – Discern

---

*V*ignette

Remember to Breathe

Anticipation was off the charts as we returned to explore a specific feature at the bottom of the ocean. Several days prior, when we were minutes from concluding our dive, a deep-sea biologist jumped up and exclaimed that we may have just discovered a new species of coral! During the extended time we spent observing this new discovery, the scientist became acutely interested in our navigation. I worked with them to ensure that we had recorded everything we needed to return to this exact spot on this specific bottom feature on the ocean floor.

As we launched our deep-sea underwater vehicle, I worked with the pilot to navigate an approach back to the spot the cameras had presented this potential new find. It seemed like forever for the vehicle to descend through the water column. Finally, we approached the ocean floor — it was time to turn on the lights, potentially revealing our revolutionary find. Anticipation and anxiety were building. The scientist next to me was super excited and very nervous. I leaned over and said, "just a few more minutes… breathe… it will help calm you".

A moment later, the lights were illuminating the ocean floor. Within ten minutes, the vehicle was back at the exact same spot where we initially spotted the coral. We were incredibly focused and intense for the next several hours. The joke between the scientist and myself was "breathe".

After the dive, the scientist thanked me for that simple piece of advice. Several days later during the expedition, there was confirmation that the coral we'd discovered was indeed a new species of Bamboo Coral and can now be found in the Smithsonian Institution. —JER

Motivation

"Motivation is a fire from within. If someone else tries to light that fire under you, chances are it will burn very briefly."
~ Stephen R. Covey

---

*V*ignette

Once more, with *Alacrity!*

What gets you up in the morning and gets you thinking, "This is a great day where I get to do ___, I will accomplish ___, I am going to contribute _____"? My mentor, Mike, asked me this question. He asked a few more questions to help me realize what I had to do to motivate the networking team. I had to find an accomplishment for the team to aspire to, while also ensuring my teammates received what was important to them for being part of the effort.

Thinking further, I realized that it wasn't so much the team's accomplishment of the goal, but more about how my teammates *felt* as they were contributing. Yes, I was aware that people had different motivations, but my epiphany was

---

the variety of what they needed to be motivated. The systems I had access to didn't provide the tools or ability to successfully motivate the team. At best, I was able to partially motivate them, but I realized later that morale was low.

Stumped, I asked my peer managers and leaders across the organization. At most, the feedback referenced policy, or detailed why the current systems and procedures are in place—not exactly what I was looking for.

After a few weeks it dawned on me—I needed to be creative and figure out a system to put in place with little-to-no support from the organization. I asked a simple question: "Why am I making such an effort for my teammates?" I felt in my heart it was the right thing, and I also understood how I should set up and support my team and this initiative so we all succeed. Then I created a motivation plan based on what I thought would help my teammates.

The motivation plan included the provisioning of money, titles, letters of accomplishment, awards, etc. But what really surprised me was the most sought-after motivator. Care to guess what that motivator is?

… A simple *thank you*. —**JER**

Among the most prominent developments in recent years in the investigation of thoughtful leadership has been the value of *motivation* for increasing organizational satisfaction, commitment, and effectiveness. Thoughtful leadership, regardless of style, can encourage and leverage an individual's motivation as well as promote the establishment and maintenance of *plane above / above the fray* transcendent leadership.

Peter Senge's (1990) book "The Fifth Discipline" introduced the benefits of a *learning organization*. Senge pointed to adaptability as a key capability for changing environments. Leaders are needed who can motivate, inspire, and promote an environment where learning is persistent and focused. The thoughtful leader seeks out opportunities to build such intentional interaction—an environment conducive for building *confidence* and *motivation*.

Thoughtful leaders encourage *ah-ha moments of discovery*— where abstract concepts come together into a solid thought.

Such moments of discovery can be considered *mental models*, providing structure for thinking and interpreting new content into long term memory, activities, and behavior.

Mental models can be likened to templates in the brain that allow the application of previous experiences to new situations, make the *unfamiliar, familiar* and it is experiential learning—*living life*—that sparks motivation and enthusiasm.

A model for creating fertile, stable ground for motivation and enthusiasm is to rally around a *common cause* of customer-focused vision. Mik Kerstin's (2018) book "Project to Product: How to Survive and Thrive in the Age of Digital Disruption with the Flow Framework" is a great resource for learning to explore this vision of flowing value to the customer. Kerstin offers a framework with measures and metrics, for how to flow value.

Transact Transform Transcend

CHAPTER FIVE

The Transactional Leader

"Effective leadership is not about making speeches or being liked; leadership is defined by results not attributes."
~ Peter F Drucker

Vignette

The Door to ... Everywhere!

I'm often asked to provide advice and counsel to the children of friends wondering which direction they should follow in school. Should they become technologists? Teachers? Engineers? Sometimes the question is, *"Should my child continue on to higher education at all?"*

"Which path is best for my child" is often the root of the question.

I tell the story of a young man—brilliant, good grades, and remarkably inventive and innovative for someone in their late teens. He had already invented several technology devices and was wondering how to best showcase his talents. He'd considered some of the best engineering universities yet was unimpressed with how they would help him transfer his innovations to the real world, or even a job.

I told him about the **hidden door.**

Simply, opportunities present themselves to those who participate. I told him to imagine traversing through the hallways and corridors of the university and passing by numerous doors and passageways. Then, imagine the same corridors with people all around, moving through but never looking, never stopping. *"You have options, stop and take a look around, see if one of those doors is for you"*, I said, *"but you have to be in the hallway to see the doors!"*

He dutifully took notes and thanked me. I suspect he wanted to get this over with so he could tell his father he had completed his assigned task with me.

"One more thing," I said.

I told him about how some doors don't appear at all unless you have certain credentials, experiences, or invitations. An assured method of getting such credentials is via college, or some type of continued education where organizations looking for folks like him can find them.

One door, for example, was a path to an internship with a large and respected tech company looking for someone just like him. *"How will they find you if you are not there?"* I asked. In order for the door to appear, you have to do more than rattle the available door handles, you have to find a way to gain access to the doors you don't initially see—remove any obstacles by being there, making yourself known in that environment, take the classes, and follow the path— *participate.* **—KER**

As previously mentioned in the thoughtful leader's journey section, most begin a path to a leadership career as a *transactional* leader. With good reason—leadership will always be about results, regardless of how well liked a leader is, how charismatic, or how caring. Aligning people, processes, and communication in an effort to create and maintain an effective, orderly, and successful organization is the goal of not just the transactional leader, but of the organization's stakeholders and participants.

To be certain, before a *thoughtful leader* can emerge—before transforming, before transcending—a leader must understand and value the relevance of the transaction, of ensuring the work of the organization is managed and completed. *How* a leader gets things done, the *artistry* of being a leader is evolutionary, but begins with a keen situational awareness of the needs of the team within the organization.

One of the great paradoxes of leadership is a transactional leader's superpower of clear, direct, and consistent communication coexisting within environments typically embroiled in chaos, ambiguity, and fear. An effective transactional leader finds a way to clear the obstacles in the path by being *flexible, practical,* and *clever.* This capability helps to ensure:

- *the organization makes the right decisions at the right time*
- *responsiveness to the needs of the organization*
- *the leader builds an inclusive and dynamic (not static) team*

Transactional leaders establish and maintain order by:

- *maximizing communication*
- *providing an effective governance structure*
- *providing a clear link between organizational activities and business requirements*
- *working to align its greatest resource: people*

Vignette

A Transactionary Tale

Reflecting on my initial leadership situations, I thought leadership was about putting the goal out there for the team, and people would do their part to earn their paycheck. Regardless if the goal was created by the team, or handed down to the team (directed), the execution by the team was the same. We are here to work, we get paid, so the team and I will accomplish the goal.

As a transactional leader, my way of framing a conversation (asking people to do things, negotiating to get results) was based on a transaction. This is what we need to do, this is how we achieve results. I'll never forget the day I truly learned what transactional leadership is all about. It's the same day I made the conscious decision to evolve into a transformational leader.

I worked for a CIO who was a traditional transactional leader. One day I was asked to help mentor one of our smart project managers (PMs) to be the leader of a newly established Project Management Office (PMO). The CIO prescribed the requirements and I set to work with the PM. For the first three weeks, we had a daily routine of training, mentoring, and leading by example. Each day I increased the involvement of the PM so that by the end of the three weeks, the PM was able to do their job as prescribed. During those three weeks, the PM and I co-created the basic process / tools for the PMO to get the initial projects documented and assigned to the engineers. The PM was doing well, the PMO was established, and we were able to integrate the PMO into Operations seamlessly.

At month two I noticed some issues. The customers and the engineers supporting the customer requirements started coming to me with complaints. I got the PM's perspective to see what we could do to resolve the growing issues. The PM was communicative and collaborative as we discussed the issues. I asked a few questions and we agreed to regroup in a few days to brainstorm. In our second meeting, I noticed a significant change in the PM's demeanor and body language. As we started to brainstorm, I realized there was a conflict of cultures (values and beliefs) and approach. The PM was very transactional in how they worked with the customers and engineers, referring to the priorities and documentation in the PMO toolset as the source of truth for getting work done and who was responsible. I was being transformational, representing and standing up for the customer's and engineer's needs. This was called a Business Process Management (BPM) approach; today we call it flowing value to the customer.

When I asked the PM who was setting the project priorities and documentation in the system, the PM said it was them. When I further inquired, the true answer was the CIO. Once a week the CIO would meet with the PM and tell the PM who was doing what, for whom, when. I asked why our agreed-upon process wasn't being used, and the PM told me it was out of their hands. After a meeting with the CIO and the executive sponsor, things stayed the same. The CIO would continue to lead how they saw fit.

Afterward, I called a meeting with the engineers. I told them the results of the meeting with the CIO. There was a long awkward silence from the engineers. Then one of the engineers spoke up and said, "You came in here, improved our quality of life. You don't dictate how to do things but ask for our opinions and let us try out our ideas, experiment with how we can best do our job."

That's when I not only realized the difference between transactional and transformational leaders, culture, mindset, etc, but made a commitment to myself to be the best transformational leader I can be. —JER

Transactional leaders plan, communicate, and build consensus for change. They are flexible and are capable of responding to ambiguity, chaos, and fear depending on the situation at hand. They:

- Understand the difference between sustaining an organization and growing it, and the impetus necessary to keep an organization vital and moving
- Understand the difference between managing and leading, and leverage the talent of the participants of the organization to drive the success of the greater organization

Vignette

Ready, Set, ... Optimize!

Leadership sent us all a message: no more raises and the hiring freeze starts *now*. In three weeks, my team and I planned to move to an advanced way of operating and wanted to hire at least one, if not two, more people. As the team and I brainstormed our future, we settled on an idea for how we could create our own roles and reorganize. The next day I gave human resources (HR) and senior leadership the proposed organizational structure and got approval.

The team's ability to rethink how to operate and sustain data center operations, coming at the problem from a different way of thinking, changing perspective, resulted in our ability to define an optimized solution for our situation. —JER

The Transactional leader excels at *appropriate communication, collaboration,* and *open discussion between the participants* of an organization. Even though wrong decisions will be made at times, the transactional leader maintains a *will to keep going,* the strength to find another way, and the dedication not to give up.

"Never give in, never give in, never, never, never."
~ Winston Churchill

Getting Work Done

Comparing Management & Leadership

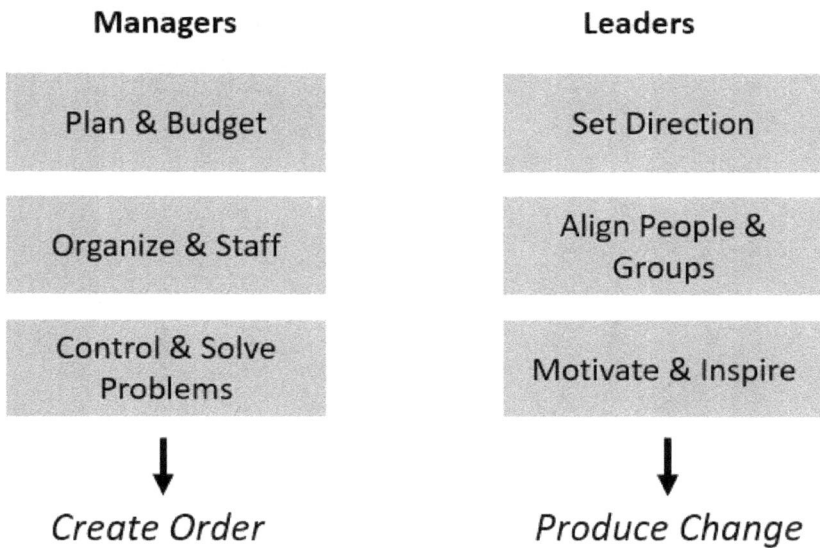

Managers

| Leaders |

Plan & Budget

Set Direction

Organize & Staff

Align People & Groups

Control & Solve Problems

Motivate & Inspire

↓

↓

Create Order

Produce Change

Portions Kotter, J.P. (2001). What leaders really do. Harvard Business Review, 79(11), 85-61.

CHAPTER SIX

The Transformational Leader

"We want a culture where it is unacceptable not to share
what you know."
~ John T. Chambers

---

*V*ignette

Charisma—Not Just for Cult Leaders

It's handy to be able to use charisma (in the popular sense of the word) to motivate and inspire followers, or to persuade, or even to regale an organization with expert oratory. But I see charisma as a tool for the leader's toolkit, something that should be brought out in times of distress, perhaps, as

---

appropriate.

Charisma is not something I'd recommend as a fundamental tool for the leader. A leader who relies too much on charisma as a main element in their persona is likely to be overwhelmed with the need to maintain power. Gardner (1990) (quoting Max Weber) had a great passage in his book: "the charismatic leader ... tends to run out of miracles ... [and] the only way to preserve power on a large scale is to organize and institutionalize", invariably moving from a strong personal charisma to a bureaucracy.

The thoughtful leader knows the difference between persona and character and knows when to open the charisma toolbox—and (more importantly) when to keep it closed. — **KER**

The transformational leader is prepared to make a *difference* in the organization. The following acronym demonstrates such a commitment—a desire (to paraphrase Steve Jobs) to make a *dent in the universe*!

This acronym evolved from working with leaders struggling to come up with new ideas encouraging new ways of thinking.

> ▶ **D—Disorient:** Does the new idea cause you to think in a new way? Does it make you tilt your head and wonder ... maybe?

▶ **E—Extend:** Does the idea extend or move along another idea or thought? Does it add something—or does it revisit something already considered?

▶ **N—Navigate:** Does the idea make it easier to understand something, see an opportunity better, and help create a path to get to where you need to be?

▶ **T—Transform:** Does the idea make you want to stop in your tracks and completely change direction?

Whether transformational or transactional, a thoughtful leader is motivated to change based on the *situational* nature of an organization's environment. Successful situational leadership requires great responsibility and skill, and "individuals alone", according to Kotter (1996), "never have all the assets needed to overcome tradition and inertia". It is the people within the organization who possess the *knowledge* and provide the talent that is the *catalyst* of the type of organization Kotter describes: "without these skills, dynamic adaptive enterprises are not possible".

The transformational leader understands the difference between "managing" and "leading" and leverages the talent of the participants of the organization to drive the success of the business (sometimes that also means being transactional or transformational, depending on the situation at hand).

Transforming means you never go back to what you were. We often talk about being ready for change, but transformation is a notch higher. It shows a level of understanding, commitment, and fortitude necessary to see things through. It raises the level for both the leader and the follower (morally, motivationally—even emotionally) to ensure new approaches and new ideas are acted upon and not left as possibilities.

A transformational leader *innovates* and *participates*—recognizing and imbuing the *valued voices* in the organization with the following:

- It's how we consume, not merely create
    - Industries are experiencing a transformational shift in how data is extracted, stored, conveyed, and even generated
- It's that we amplify, not merely administer
    - Put more simply, a generation ago, the most popular job for a data person was the DBA, the database administrator; it's no longer adequate to be merely an administrator of data
    - Today we're asking more from our data than static reports of last month's numbers, or even yesterday's reports—we are asking for insight & wisdom

- It's when we collide (our unexpected ah-ha moments of discovery)
- Power (or value) is in what you share, not merely what you know

What you will find when you evolve from a transactional to transformational leader is that you'll have more opportunity and ability to succeed across a greater range of situations and organizations. This increase in success is due to being plugged in at a greater level, more immersed than a transactional leader. Why? Because you are leading and facilitating the communicating, collaborating, and creating the vision and working to make it a reality.

Contributing to the vision is an essential responsibility for the transformational leader—as is *transparency*. A thoughtful leader brings transparency into and across the organization and its ecosystem of vendors / partners so everyone works from the same data, empowered to have and share ideas, and everyone has access to what they need when they need it. This is the true responsibility and at the core of what it takes and means to be a transformational leader.

Transact Transform Transcend

CHAPTER SEVEN

The Transcendent Leader

"There will be blind alleys and one-night wonders and soul-crushing jobs and wake-up calls and crises of confidence and moments of transcendence when you are walking down the street, and someone will thank you for telling your story because it resonated with their own."
~ Lin-Manuel Miranda

Vignette

I Can Fly Twice as High

I remember a role where I had to be more pragmatic and collaborative (a large international divestiture where many of us had shared leadership responsibilities and we needed

---

to solve problems quickly between offices in the US and Australia). Our work was task-driven and very transactional, but there was time for influencing, connecting, and helping others strive (transform) for more than what they had thought possible.

There was something more occurring, however. More than transactional or even transformational. In fact, it was— **transcendent**.

I began using a phrase that has become *yet another* Ken-ism: *the plane above*.

It simply refers to the requirement to lift ourselves out of / above whatever our current tactical / transactional situation and begin to consider the work at hand in a new way. Even a quick break to consider an alternate perspective or merely taking a moment to stop, look up above the fray, and address issues and problems without the burden of being hyper-focused or overwhelmed enables an understanding— a transcendence—to *the plane above* level of analysis, an option to access a different part of yourself previously unknown. —**KER**

The *transcendent leader* is different.

A transcendent leader helps organizations make the right decisions at the right time, but what makes a transcendent leader different from other leadership efforts?

An experienced leader will likely recognize a multitude of *options* available for achieving equally good and desired results. *Option A,* for example, may be to implement a goal faster with less regard for cost containment. *Option B* may be to take a slower route to achieving a goal but saving money in the process. Each could be viable. Options are a bit challenging for the transactional leader (perhaps too few options—limited and focused explicitly on the tasks at hand), and for the transformational leader, options may be considered distractions after all of the collisions and discoveries (at this point, transforming what you have into something else is like having a jigsaw puzzle with all of the pieces finally spread out, turned right side up, with maybe a few of the corner pieces already in place—ready to be assembled in just the right way—and others wanting to toss a box of new pieces of an entirely different puzzle into the mix).

But for the transcendent leader, any situation, any opportunity, any task, can be filled with options. Such is the nature of the translatory nature in all we do. For the thoughtful leader, this is crucial since it helps underscore the value of meaning, and that merely applying a single methodology to a variety of problems is not likely to work.

Options ... it's always good to have options!

The transcendent leader understands the difference between sustaining an organization and growing it—and is the impetus that keeps an organization vital and moving. While a transcendent leader leverages all the skills and attributes of both transactional and transformational leaders, the transcendent leader stays *above the fray*. As detailed in the vignette above, it's an easy concept, yet harder to maintain as a leader.

Noblesse Oblige

The noble obligation of those of high rank to be honorable and generous.

Duty, Obligation, Responsibility—the social force that binds you to the courses of action demanded by that force; "we must instill a sense of duty in our children"; "every right implies a responsibility; every opportunity, an obligation; every possession, a duty"
~ John D. Rockefeller Jr.

"I define a leader as anyone who takes responsibility for finding the potential in people and processes, and who has the courage to develop that potential."
~ Brené Brown

Transcendent leaders approach their responsibilities with a full understanding of the *obligation* accompanying their position. A heightened sense of duty, honor, and an innate sense of doing what is right. Here is a quick list of traits recognizable in the thoughtful leader:

- Helps organizations *understand*, develop, and leverage core capabilities
- Leads organizations to be *inclusive,* not exclusionary and static
- Analyzes the *impact* (including change in behavior) that often occurs as a result of *senior leadership* change
- Evaluates the *actions* of leaders placed into new situations

Contrast this with generations approaching leadership as a *reward* for hard work, *personal recompense* for working long hours and scratching or clawing their way to the top. Can a thoughtful leader exist in an organization that empowers and values the *me-first* leader? Not for long, and not without suffering from politics, jockeying for position, and being pressured to play "the game". A thoughtful leader will also be pressed to make quick decisions without the time to consider if it's the best decision for their team and whether it truly aligns with their values.

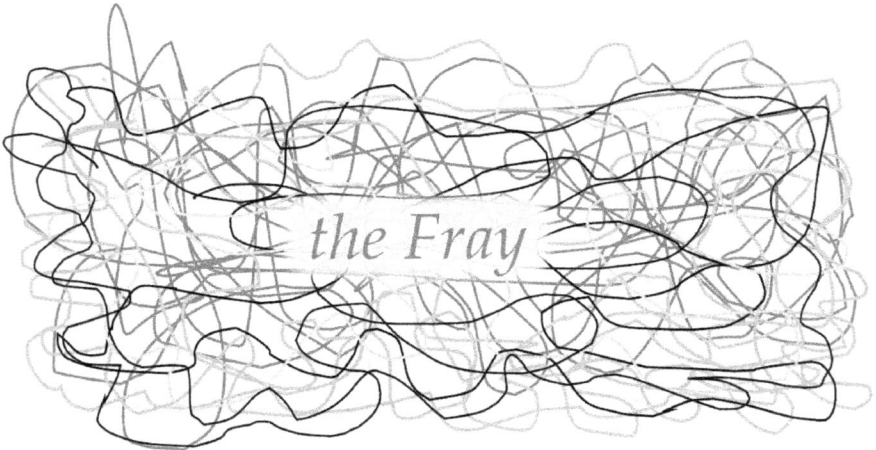

The *fray* (the activity churning around us, whether tasks or transformations) tends to require our focus—so much, to the point of hyperfocus at times. Being *above the fray* requires more mental dexterity than physical prowess or attendance.

Learning to be a transcendent leader requires appropriate communication, collaboration, and open discussion between the *participants* of an organization. Keeping things transcendent means that even though wrong decisions will be made at times, the organization maintains a will to keep going, the strength to find another way, and the dedication not to give up.

Becoming a *plane above / above the fray* transcendent leader involves getting managers to start lifting themselves out of whatever situation they're in to start thinking about their work in a new way. Whether via alternate perspectives or just looking at what they do from an external view—helping someone think about their issues and problems without being inculcated in historical, emotional, or functional attachment allows them to understand "the plane above" level of analysis. This type of approach is transcendent and allows a leader access to a different part of him / herself that was previously unknown.

Transact Transform Transcend

CHAPTER EIGHT

Making the Unfamiliar Familiar

"My brain is only a receiver, in the Universe there is a core from which we obtain knowledge, strength and inspiration. I have not penetrated into the secrets of this core, but I know that it exists."
~ Nikola Tesla

"Transcendence refers to the very highest and most inclusive or holistic levels of human consciousness, behaving and relating, as ends rather than means, to oneself, to significant others, to human beings in general, to other species, to nature, and to the cosmos."
~ Abraham Maslow

Vignette

The Leader of Requirement

The most effective leader harnesses both the right and left sides of the brain, develops it, and learns to recognize situations where a more creative approach is required (dealing with employees or negotiating a contract, for example), and feeling just as at ease playing the role of the hard-nose, number crunching manager when the situation calls for it.

The most telling weakness of not having high Emotional Intelligence was described well by Goleman (1999) when he was retelling the story of the executive humbled by an experience overseas. He was not able to see how others viewed him and probably existed as a *leader* for years without ever realizing there was an entirely different plane of existence (empathy) he was missing.

The good news is that the five elements of Emotional Intelligence can be *nurtured* and taught; the bad news is that many executives don't even know how to think about such things. If they do, they often imagine themselves *doing okay* since few are brave enough to say otherwise. I like Goleman's quote: *"He went home and told his family—but they only confirmed what he'd heard at work. When their opinions on any given subject did not mesh with his, they, too, were frightened of him."* Frightened? I wonder how many executives think they are good at leading organizations, fair to their employees, and open to new ideas—but in reality, are just big bad ogres (apologies to Shrek)?

As with any approach to leadership, balance is probably key when comparing left and right brain tendencies. The executive capable of adroitly moving between a closed door cost-cutting session to a company picnic where they engage with all the employees, and does so with authenticity, is a preferred leader in my view. Those that *fake* their way through one side or the other are the ones in most need of assistance.

I liked Goleman's discussion around the various parts of the brain that govern the creative and logical responses we have (limbic and neocortex). It shows that it is possible for the thoughtful leader (or anyone) to exercise their brains to overcome deficiencies. It may not turn a "Bartleby" into a "Falstaff", but it can show a leader how to fine tune his or her craft, and become more effective. —**KER**

One of the bigger challenges for a transcendent and thoughtful leader is to develop core foundational values and beliefs centered on *energy*. Why? Energy-based thinking and doing has been considered negative, too ethereal, or encumbered by other social stigmas. It can be difficult to find a good, valid source of information about energy and, more specifically, a leader's unique interaction with energy.

Advances in quantum science are providing us with *validation* of ancient wisdoms, information from past centuries, and newfound knowledge and understanding of the universe around us. The deeper today's quantum scientists go into the world of quantum, the more they validate energy as the building blocks of the universe. Energy is at the very core of the foundation for life as we know it, which brings about more mystery and unknowns.

To evolve and develop as a transcendent leader, you must understand and believe in the energetic connection you have with the universe. Accepting and connecting with your ability to energetically connect with others, with tangible physical objects, and even with (commonly accepted) intangible things in the universe will help differentiate you from other leaders.

Intuition

"Being able to put your blinders on, ignore negative opinions, and follow your strong intuition is what's validating to me. It's a great feeling to know you can trust your gut."
~ Whitney Wolfe Herd

Another way to think of intuition is that this direct knowledge is essentially a download of information from all of our senses into our brain. It occurs when we stop thinking and analyzing and we go into quiet *contemplation* and *reflection*. According to Dispenza (2017), it's almost as if our brain pauses, and that pause in the chatter allows other types of information to enter our nervous system. The challenge most of us face is what to do with the information when we receive it.

While science does not yet completely understand intuition (it's not merely magic!), more and more studies are being developed to help us not only understand how it works, but how to measure it.

Intuition and the Thoughtful Leader

Can your Intuition help you become a more Thoughtful Leader?

Absolutely

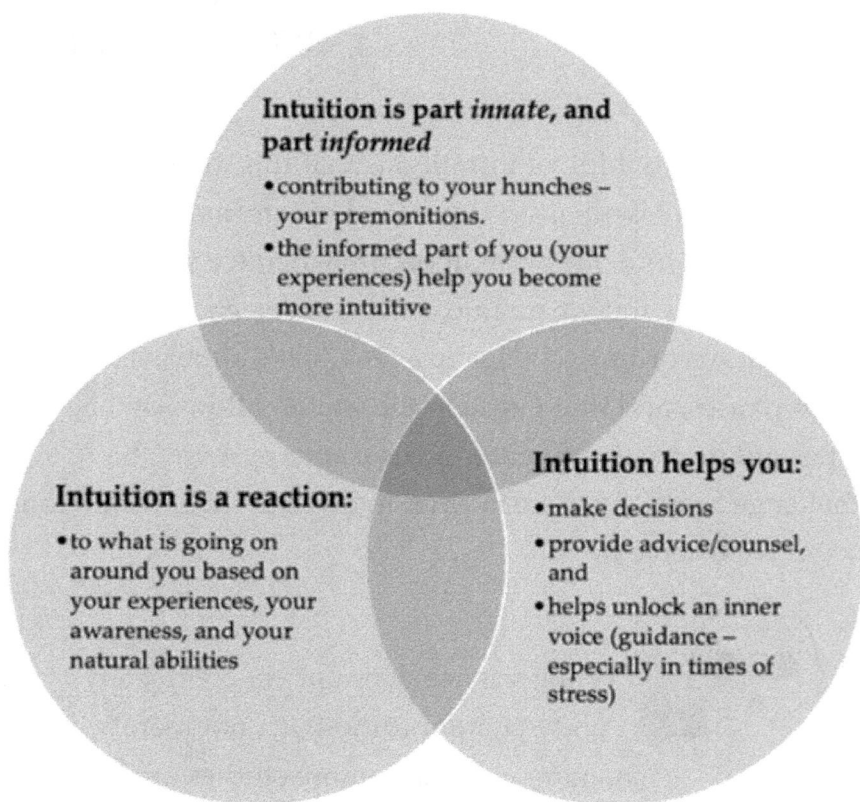

Intuition is part *innate*, and part *informed*

- contributing to your hunches – your premonitions.
- the informed part of you (your experiences) help you become more intuitive

Intuition is a reaction:

- to what is going on around you based on your experiences, your awareness, and your natural abilities

Intuition helps you:

- make decisions
- provide advice/counsel, and
- helps unlock an inner voice (guidance – especially in times of stress)

Vignette

Intuition Cognition

The leader of our team on a high-profile transformation of the US Corporate Headquarters for a globally recognized brand, handed me a report and asked what I thought. The transformation was going poorly, and we had just received a call that lawyers were going to be involved. As I scanned the report, my *intuition* and *gut* feelings were telling me the data was wrong. However, when you looked up the information within the trusted sources, the information matched. I told my leader how I felt and was told to investigate and see what I could come up with. For the next two days I searched but nothing I had access to or that was published would verify my feelings.

A few years later I ran into a former employee who had been involved with the high-profile transformation on the customer side. As we reminisced and caught up, they asked, "How did you know the report was incorrect?"

I smiled and said, "You may not believe this, but my intuition told me this was wrong and provided me with the information I submitted in my response to the report." Now it was the former employee who smiled back at me and said, "I wish I had those skills, because you nailed it... you were right." —**JER**

Thoughtful leaders, in addition to having the experience, knowledge, and tools of the transactional, transformational, and the transcendent leader, have an enabling attribute ... *something more*. Something deep inside compelling a deeper analysis, a more universal understanding and an evaluation of both environment and possibilities. Earlier, this was referred to as: *awakened to opportunities, imagination, and the possibilities of "what if"*.

Another way to think of this is as an ability to *perceive*. Finding a way to make the *unfamiliar ... familiar*. A perception that there are multiple perspectives regarding what and why things happen, that we can *feel* our way by simply knowing or going along with the momentum or flow of what is happening in the environment around us.

Transact Transform Transcend

CHAPTER NINE

LEAD

"Hear with your heart and you won't hear a sound."
~ *Neil Sedaka / Howard Greenfield*

As described earlier, a thoughtful leader—at their core:

- *Listens*—not just with their ears, but with their heart, their experiences, and with an *informed gut*

- **Empathizes** with their team—taking the time to lean in and share experiences, pay attention to the epidata swirling around everyone, and being aware of what is going on within the organization

- *Absorbs* and synthesizes activities and happenings all around

- *Discerns*, participates, and doesn't retreat—taking the time to comprehend and consider the whole environment and possibilities

These four words, of course, make up the mnemonic / acronym **LEAD**. This section will focus on these four specific traits of a thoughtful leader and the thoughtfulness that emerges from within *yourself.*

*V*ignette

The *Rest* of the Story

A few years back a much-adored professional basketball team ended up relocating from one city to another. Much of the discussion in the press was about how the current city/community couldn't support the team—it was simple, they said, the team was losing money, and a move was inevitable.

What no one heard was the *real* reason.

Specifically, the decline and the *moral mistake* made by the owner of the team a few years prior.

Until the team owner was scandalized for sexual misconduct, the team enjoyed great success, often leading the league in attendance, and becoming *the place to be* in the city on game nights.

A simple survey would likely show the decline in support for the team began *after* the scandal broke, yet that was never really discussed. Today, we'd call it *quiet quitting*. Fans just stopped participating.

It's common, it seems, that people can speak loudly and convincingly … often without having to say anything out loud. In this case they spoke with their wallets. —**KER**

Listen

As previously described, one of the hallmarks of being a *thoughtful leader* is being able to move successfully in the *above the fray* space, being able to lift your eyes up and say, *"OK, there's more than just what I'm doing at this particular moment."* Being an active participant within an organization is more critical than tasks that you have. Experience makes you more aware, motivated, and resilient. Most thoughtful leaders are *nurtured*, not merely *born*. A leader becomes thoughtful through experience, *battle tested* when faced with the crises within any organization.

$V_{ignette}$

Listening in the Deep

My teammates and I were on patrol, punching holes in the ocean as we called it, listening to the ocean through our headsets as we stood our watch aboard our submarine. We had been on station for a few weeks now and everyone had settled into a routine. As I was about to chime into a conversation, I stopped, closed my eyes, and listened. What was that? What was I hearing? There was something there, but I was unsure of what it was. After a few seconds, I realized that what I was hearing was not making sense. It was something I shouldn't be hearing underwater. What the heck?

Another time, I was listening to a conversation between a Windows administrator and a UNIX administrator. The two administrators had come to me independently, complaining and wanting me to talk to their counterpart. I asked that they write down an agenda with their key points and have a conversation... to listen to what the other has to say. The conversation started on neutral terms but then got heated. As I was thinking to myself, this is not making sense, I found myself instinctually putting myself physically in between the two administrators, sending one to the office and the other home to cool down. I said we'd pick this up in the morning.

What do these two experiences have in common? While

listening, I found myself confused and disoriented—not hearing what I expected to hear, not understanding the cause, source, why I was hearing the sounds and information coming from what / whom I was listening to.

The sound transmitted underwater into the ocean, traveling through the water, being detected and processed by our sonar system, and I was hearing in my headphones was Madonna's song *Like a Virgin* followed by Bruce Springsteen's song *Born In The USA*. (It wasn't until almost two decades later when I heard about the John Walker spy ring scandal. I think the information John Walker provided resulted in American music being transmitted underwater.)

The next morning when the administrators and I had a follow up meeting, we all realized that the conflict was a combination of pride, ego, and misunderstanding. The good news is that we were able to align and agree on the path forward.

What I learned from these and several other listening experiences is that to listen, you have to let go of your expectations, let go of your predictions, quiet yourself, and learn to be in the moment. What I've found is the more I purely listen, the better I am at understanding, and the quicker I am able to react with the proper response.

It's easy to let my preconceptions get in the way of taking in the reality of what's happening right now, process, and respond. I also realized, when I FEEL disoriented, that's a

> good thing. It means I'm being provided an opportunity to hear something new for the first time, to learn, and grow. — **JER**

A helpful learning mnemonic is the acronym: **LISTEN**.

Listening is perhaps the most important tool for a thoughtful leader. A thoughtful leader listens authentically, taking time to absorb what is happening all around.

L—Learn

Try to learn as much as you can about as much as you can, from others, from the environment, from your team—learn from everything that's around you.

I—Interpret

Take what you have learned and use it to interpret what it means and represents for your organization, and for the individuals on your team.

S—Shape

Everyone around you will tend to gravitate to what they know; learn to help them shape what they know and bring new ideas and new ways of thinking to the organization

T —Transform

Be ready for transformation, not mere change (where things may also change back or revert to the way things were). Be ready to transform the organization and go a new direction instead of just going the same old way.

E—Evolve

Evolution occurs when you're effective at all these things. A thoughtful leader evolves.

N—Nurture

Take the time and the opportunity to nurture your team; help them along, stay connected and engage them with regular conversations. A thoughtful leader is always ready to nurture next.

Empathy

"You are more than the sum of the people you've met along the way, especially those you've met at particular intersections at a specific moment in your life. Good or bad, all you've done before this has prepared you for right now."

~ Van Sachs

Vignette

Lead Me to the Music

I was 15 and looking for something to do. My high school had an internship program and introduced me to an amazing world of opportunity for a kid looking to do, well … anything! I was interested in music and was placed with Mary, the manager of a local music store in Charlotte.

Technically, the internship was for business operations, so I spent a lot of time with Mary in the back office, learning how a music store worked (supply chain, vendor relations, consignments, etc.). But she took an interest in me. I can't tell you why (maybe because I was a curious 15-year-old!), but she let me *experiment* and *explore* all of the roles at the store.

One week I'd be with Don, learning not just to fix, but to *repair* guitars (there IS a difference he'd tell me, and that I had to *pay attention to more than what we were told* about a particular instrument).

The next week I'd be with Van, *learning by listening* to the customers walking in—what they wanted, what their musical aspirations were.

Mary was an amazing leader. Perhaps my best evidence of that is that she remains in my direct memory—a straight line to those days of watching her manage by walkabout, *empathizing* with all the customers, and *genuinely* taking the time with the most novice to the most experienced.

She was the first to teach me about the *value of relationships* (not just the technical expertise of whatever the store was selling, but how the customer wanted to use the gear).

Relationships mattered. Mary was a natural at *balancing* product expertise and meaningful relationships.

While Mary wasn't a musician herself, she understood the *language of music* and was able to interact with and talk with customers in a language they understood. And she was willing to give a 15 year old me an opportunity to have those talks with her, to see and experience all aspects of a dynamic interconnected community.

I think that's the key for emerging leaders—having opportunities to experience and experiment. And in a music store on top of that! Who would have thought—learning to be a leader while playing with guitars! —**KER**

"One of the criticisms I've faced over the years is that I'm not aggressive enough or assertive enough, or maybe somehow, because I'm empathetic, it means I'm weak. I totally rebel against that. I refuse to believe that you cannot be both compassionate and strong."
~ *Jacinda Ardern*

Vignette

Feeling Your Way to Empathy

During the year 2023 I witnessed more articles and book authors making calls for a leader to have empathy or be empathetic than the prior decade combined. This led me to deeply reflect within myself and evaluate my understanding of what empathy is and how to provide empathy to others.

What I found—what resonated with me—was the experiential nature of the word empathy. As a noun or subject that I had to understand, and as a verb that I had to take action by conveying my understanding. The metric for success was to ask a single question: "Did the individual feel that I understood?"

In order to succeed with being empathetic, I had to focus inside to the connection of the situation within. Next I had to transfer what I was feeling to the person / team. I realized the more genuine and true I was to my interpersonal connection, the more of an increase, or as Ken would say, an *amplification* of conviction, being felt by the person / team.

This led to the realization that my feelings, what I felt and what the person or team felt, was the foundation or core of the ability to understand what empathy is and how to be

> empathic or provide empathy. The amount of conviction was directly dependent upon the authenticity or genuineness associated with the feelings which aligns to the common thread of amplification found throughout this book. —JER

Daniel Goleman (1998) details several elements of the "emotional intelligence" of leaders, focusing on neurological links to intelligence and leadership. He describes *empathy* as a skill, an ability that helps connect to the emotional architecture of individuals—a skill enabling someone to divine insight from behaviors and interactions. Such an awareness and skill could be helpful to a leader endeavoring to build and retain talent, increase sensitivity to the cultural needs of an organization, and elevate the level of service to customers and partners.

The empathetic leader addresses the ever-changing requirements surrounding today's leader and manager issues. Learning to be an empathetic leader requires appropriate communication, collaboration, and an open discussion between the participants of an organization. *Keeping things empathetic* means understanding the difference between sustaining an organization and growing it, and provides the impetus that keeps an organization vital and moving.

The universal truth here is that you can't just have empathetic relationships only when something is needed—it must be built, maintained, and endured because they come from authentic genuine concern. This includes listening authentically, including a balance that comes from being sincere—and not driven just by personal gain.

An empathetic leader creates an environment that endures beyond typical relationship roles—and knows empathy is a skill that can't be pulled out of a leader toolkit a couple of times a year. True empathy comes from persistent, consistent, and bi-directional communication.

Absorb

"We should all endeavor to become one on whom nothing is lost"
~ Henry James

Vignette

Be a Sponge!

My captain asked if I could fix a program which was months behind schedule and overrun on the budget. I said yes, but fixing the program would mean going against the current political powers and some power brokers would not be happy. The captain looked me in the eye and said, "Fix it." The first step? Meet face-to-face with the program's strongest and biggest blocker to *listen*. Second was to gather the leaders of seven key organizations, bring them in a room, align, and agree. The result? We defined a standard and metrics for operational certification and approval. Our third step was updating the program by absorbing the disparate data points, ideas, solutions, and key personnel. We succeeded in getting the program back on track to meet its target dates — and it came in under budget. The program went operational and became a US Navy standard supporting global operations and assets for many years.

Years later I was asked by one of my mentors and the Vice President of Professional Services, to fix the deployment problem with our product. My mind flashed back to working with the captain and team as we fixed the program. The path forward was very similar so I went out into the field and visited our global partners deploying our product abroad to *listen* to what they had to say. A clear picture formed as I listened. Just like the program, defining an industry standard was a key element. With the standard defined, I worked with global system integrators to standardize the installation and configuration. Once the global system integrator channel was up and running with trained system integrators working in sync with our professional services teams from around the world, the deployment problems dissipated and we moved onto solving support challenges.

For both experiences, the *ability to absorb* was critical to our success. As I reflect on my leadership journey, I realize that my ability to absorb is at the heart and soul of my ascending to be a transcendent leader. Just as my teammates from around the world were able to absorb, I too have to absorb what is going on in the environment, the people around me, my conscious self, and inner self to become one. —JER

Absorb is about being a *collector*—a collector of ideas, technologies, perspectives—anything, really. Being able to *recognize* and *consume* new approaches and possibilities unlocks a willingness to consider even more possibilities. Sometimes new, often something recycled or reconsidered, but absorb is about *listening* and *learning* as much as you can—about *as much as you can*.

Often, absorb is about the mundane. Paying attention and being ready to help the organization control costs, manage resources, and negotiate agreements comes from having absorbed *data*, *information*, and *knowledge* over the course of a career. A thoughtful leader, however, can do more—much more.

A thoughtful leader absorbs more than what is required for a specific task or job. They understand, for example, the possibilities, opportunities, and value of new ideas. They also know and understand that *not all ideas are good for the organization* at a given time. The old adage comes to mind: **just because you can doesn't mean you should**. The thoughtful (and absorbing) leader puts this type of *insight* and *wisdom* to good use by focusing attention on *innovation*.

Establishing an environment that values innovation is a great way to build capabilities, promote resilience, and foster relationships that can turn a vendor into a true partner.

Following is an acronym for INNOVATE:

▶ **I—Investigate:** Explore and research new ideas or concepts.

▶ **N—Navigate:** Possibilities, partnerships, and explore new environments for creativity and experimentation.

▶ **N—Network:** Connect with others in your field to exchange knowledge and collaborate on innovative projects.

▶ **O—Originate:** Embrace different perspectives and coalesce learning and findings into original work and new possibilities.

▶ **V—Vision:** Develop a clear vision of the desired outcome or innovative solution.

▶ **A—Adapt:** Be flexible and willing to adjust approaches as needed.

▶ **T—Test:** Ensure innovations are repeatable, reproducible, and translatable while exploring, experiencing, and learning from both failures and successes.

▶ **E—Extend:** Put your innovative ideas into action.

A culture of innovation can help with *organizational clarity* as well, providing a space for considering new and possibly seductive technologies, processes, and solutions. Instead of avoiding the next new thing (or shiny red object), a space for innovation can provide a testing area to evaluate, consider, and test next generation possibilities—a deliberate and meaningful place to absorb and develop expertise.

An opportunity to experiment can be invaluable. Consider the popular perennial leadership paradox of aligning both the *growth* and the *cost containment* goals of an organization.

Leaders are asked to reduce costs in core areas while simultaneously providing routes to growth in revenue:

- A *transactional* leader will likely cut costs in one area to put it in another.
- A *transforming* leader will likely find ways to drive investment in other areas, growing and reducing the need for deep cuts.
- A *transcendent* leader will likely find an entirely new source of funding, an alternate resource, or drive value in an entirely different way.

Leaders (of any style) with the intent and resolve to commit to innovation as a core *organizational currency* will grow absorption throughout the organization—establishing methods for containing costs, accelerating time to revenue, and reducing operational ambiguity / drift.

Innovation is often about rediscovery and the value generated by an incumbent team— *absorbing* the stories of innovation out there and adding (and sharing) throughout the organization.

Many leaders will set up labs, testing centers, and R&D facilities to facilitate and promote innovation within their organizations. But innovation *doesn't have to occur in a physical space*. On the contrary, a culture of innovation is most effective when it becomes part of the *mindset* of an organization.

Discern

"The best leaders are readers of people. They have the intuitive ability to understand others by discerning how they feel and recognizing what they sense."
~ John C. Maxwell

---

*V*ignette

A Degree or Two Can Make All the Difference

It was during the cold war period, I was a Sonar Technician on watch, "on the stack in the shack" as we called it, aboard a US Navy Fast Attack Submarine. We were on patrol, when I suddenly heard something. After a few minutes, something felt different so we sent one of our team mates to inform the signal specialist. When the signal specialist arrived, he plugged his headphones into the stack and started listening. There was a very long, awkward, and highly anticipative silence. In less than a minute, the signal specialist asked if we had started recording what was happening. "Yes," we replied. He said, "Good, now let's go wake up the captain."

For the next two hours, the sub was in a heightened state of awareness. Like you see in the movies, any unnecessary activities were stopped and everyone was quiet.

After the event was over, which just so happened to be about the time our sonar watch was ending, the signal specialist pulled our sonar watch team aside and debriefed us on what had just transpired. What I did not realize at the time, was that I had just experienced an advanced lesson in how to observe and be perceptive.

Throughout the event, during this debrief, and at random moments in the upcoming weeks and months ahead, my sonar watch team and I experienced firsthand how the signal specialist used heightened awareness and observation skills to discern. In the moment, while the event was transpiring in real time, the signal specialist worked with a vast array of crew members of various ranks. After the event, the signal specialist worked with even more Navy officers and personnel. The common behavior and leadership result was that everyone witnessing the event was asked about what they were sensing and feeling, while everyone hearing about the event after the fact was asked what they sensed or felt.

About a year later while on travel, I ran into the signal specialist who was onto another assignment. When he asked how I was doing, I reached into my bag and pulled out my headphones, which were the same make and model he brought into the sonar shack a year ago for me to use. We both laughed and he provided one of the best compliments I have received to date: "Your ability to sense and feel what is going on, the speed at which you can process to successfully lead others in reacting, doing the right thing is phenomenal."

Several years later as an IT Director, leading a manufacturing company's IT Team, the mainframe failed, production was halted, and every minute of downtime was a loss in revenue. My mind took me back to the leadership example provided by the signal specialist, and I relived those lessons learned. I did not realize it at the moment, but this would be my first big opportunity to pay it forward and pass it along to others... "it" being heightened awareness and observation skills and how to discern. —**JER**

"The supreme end of education is expert discernment in all things — the power to tell the good from the bad, the genuine from the counterfeit, and to prefer the good and the genuine to the bad and the counterfeit."
~ *Samuel Johnson*

Referencing the data model illustrated in the insight and wisdom section, it is not by accident that *discern* is the next level in the progression of data analytics. Discerning direction and decisions from wisdom, tangible (as well as intangible) data requires *experience*, a standard of *truth, moral / ethical* grounding, and a commitment to *listening*. This harnesses a powerful combination of skill that enable the thoughtful leader to *rise above the fray* and operate at a higher level of *clarity* and *vision*. This is why in the table of leadership styles in A Thoughtful Leader's Journey section the ability to Discern is the *superpower* for the Transcendent Leader.

One of the most significant acronyms in this book is **LEAD** because it contains an important theme woven throughout this book which is "D" for Discern. The ability to discern is the key enabler for a transactional or transformational leader to ascend or lead as a transcendent leader.

The transcendent leader retrieves and receives information from many sources. Some are tangible sources like a database, newspaper, or a person. However, some are intangible sources like the vibe of a meeting, how one may react to an event, or how one may feel about an individual but cannot explain *why* they feel the way they do.

The ability to discern is the key enabler for a transactional or transformational leader to ascend or lead as a transcendent leader.

Transact Transform Transcend

CHAPTER TEN

Addressing Cultural Debt

"The woods are lovely, dark and deep, but I have promises
to keep, and miles to go before I sleep."

~ Robert Frost

Vignette

A Shadow of a (Cultural) Debt

People tend to gravitate to what they know. Worse, sometimes individuals become stagnant with what they know, failing to stay current and putting an organization at risk.

I've met too many folks like this who acquire skills and experience only to let them *evaporate* over time. Usually this is because they've found a position that suits them, one that

---

requires little motivation for continuing to grow. The common denominator is usually a focus on self (or self-preservation) and with little regard to the needs of the organization.

One such fellow, the software team leader, was charismatic and embedded in a position of power on a software development team and causing actual ruin to the organization.

I was asked to evaluate the team — they were missing deadlines, arguing with their contractors, and generally avoiding making progress on a critical system upgrade. My analysis was quick and revelatory: the team leader didn't want ANY changes … at all! He sought to shut down any attempt to change his comfortable environment, to the point of continuing to advocate for old development environments and programming languages and (dangerous) unpatchable older operating systems.

Because of his status, he was able to create a *culture* where he was respected as the smartest in the room, the most experienced, and the most connected to leadership. He was able to tamp down any attempts of innovation and technology evolution as well. The members of the team were made to feel their training, their experiences, and successes with modern development tools were a bad fit for his special and unique environment.

Such individuals either fell in line or were forced out of the organization.

This type of environment can't exist for long, but the real damage can cause a significant *cultural debt*. In this case, fixing the problem required a wholesale change of the internal team to an external managed service provider—a fiscal debt. The more significant damage was to the development team members, those close to the working environments, and to the general organizational health.

The organization is now stable and working with modern (and more secure) software, but the all powerful software team leader, finally removed, had cast a large shadow—leaving behind those remaining to deal with broken relationships, anxiety, and trust issues. —**KER**

Most will recognize the term *technical debt* and what it represents to an organization. A quick description would be the cost of technology assets (software, hardware, solutions, etc.) that are still on the books but are no longer valued as much as before. Perhaps such assets are being retired, sunsetted, or replaced in favor of some newer (or more effective) solution. It can also be critical infrastructure built on outdated equipment or solutions that would require significant effort or downtime to replace. *Fiscal debt* is a more general and overarching term and can refer to the monetary / capital debts of an organization.

An organization's *cultural debt* includes the broken promises of projects that never came to fruition, the wounds from seemingly endless reorganization efforts, and (especially) the *espoused* versus *the real* (what is *said to be* in an organization, against what *really happens*). Cultural debt is a bit more unusual, perhaps novel to consider in most organizations, and more nuanced—but it is always present and must be considered.

Remember our earlier description of *organizational awareness*? It's the practice of helping organizations discover, optimize, and mature their ever-evolving work environments. Organization awareness assesses an organization's *tolerance for change, ability to absorb new information,* and *history* in an effort to determine the overall readiness for change. It addresses the *structure of an organization,* its *governance, culture, politics,* and *espoused vs. in place* processes.

As we mentioned before, an organization's *history,* particularly their *in-place, evolved-over-time* culture is overlooked. This is often referred to as the difference between what is *espoused* (what is *said* to be factual) and what is *real* (what *is* factual). Typically manifested in a cycle of change that may be better called a cycle of *"what the heck?!"* change because it recurs so often in organizations.

Here is a quick visual description:

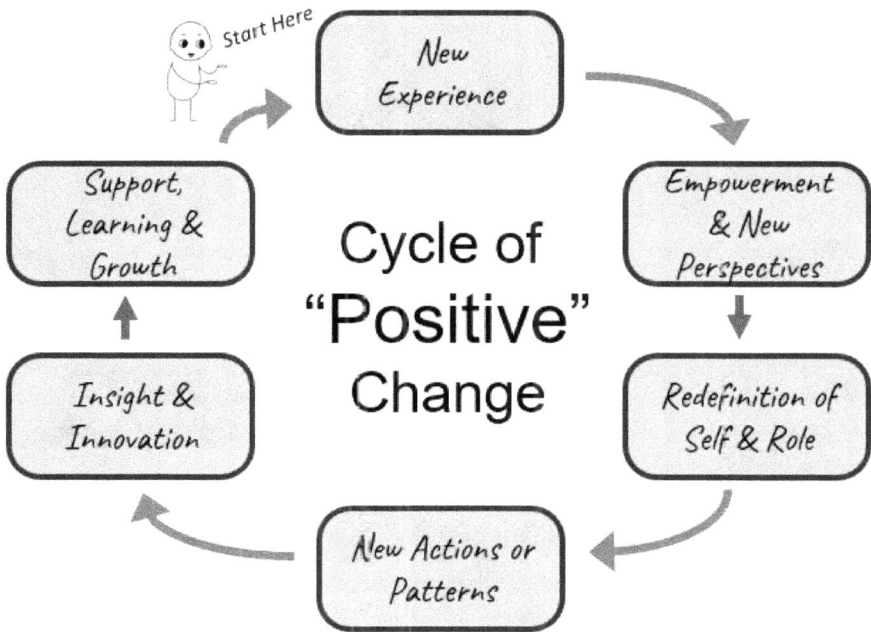

Start Here

New
Experience

Empowerment
& New
Perspectives

Cycle of
"Positive"
Change

Support,
Learning &
Growth

Redefinition of
Self & Role

Insight &
Innovation

New Actions or
Patterns

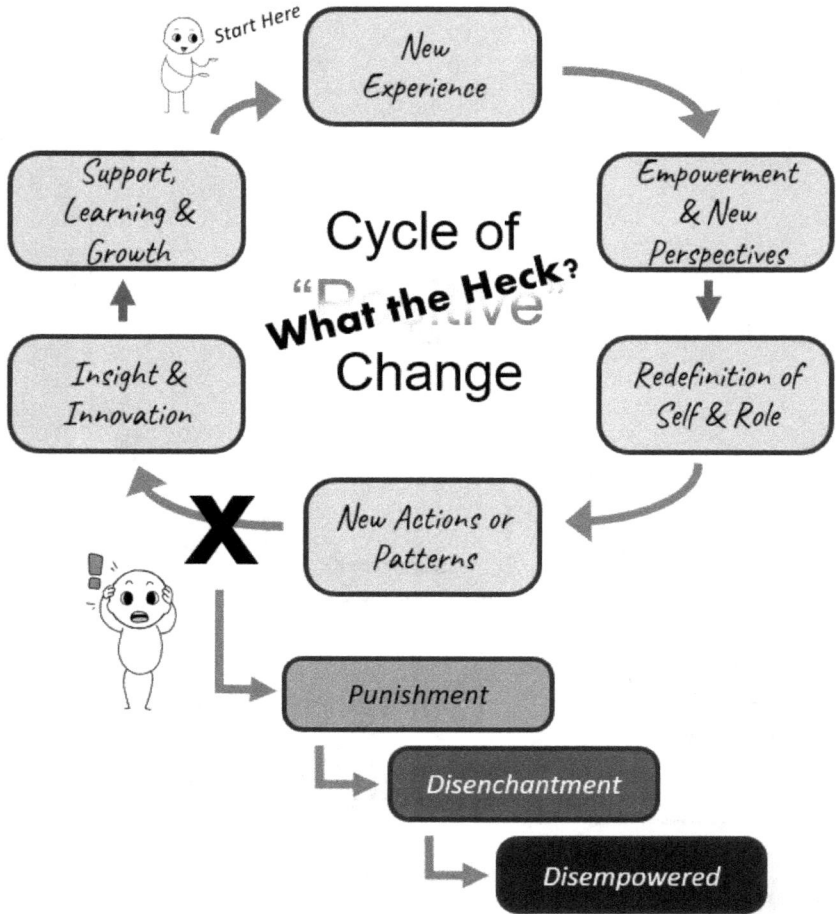

Start Here

New Experience

Support, Learning & Growth

Empowerment & New Perspectives

Cycle of "Positive Change"

What the Heck?

Insight & Innovation

Redefinition of Self & Role

New Actions or Patterns

Punishment

Disenchantment

Disempowered

In this example, things start on a great note, as most projects and initiatives do. The cycle continues and *empowerment and new perspectives* develop and begin to emerge. Excitement and organizational growth continue with *redefinition of self & role*, along with *new actions or patterns*. Although things can go awry at any point along the cycle of change, it's often the point of *committing* to new patterns—but before actually *implementing* anything—that things unravel.

The reasons for such denouements are many and varied, of course. Typical reasons for such abrupt changes are financial concerns, talent/resource capabilities, or even fear of the unknown. However, when the rug is pulled from under any organizational effort, people may become upset and disenchanted—do that enough times in an organization and animosity builds up, creating a *debt* which means when it's time to go back and start a new project the team will not believe it. They're not going to have that same enthusiasm that is required to do something amazing.

Punishment turns into disenchantment and ultimately disempowerment. The cycle of *"what the heck?!"* change never gets to that *support, learning,* and *growth* phase so critical for organizations wanting to grow and mature to a new level.

Transact Transform Transcend

CHAPTER ELEVEN

Final Thoughts

"Pursue some path, however narrow and crooked, in which you can walk with love and reverence."

~ Henry David Thoreau

Vignette

The Struggle is Real

I've come to realize this period of my life and career is all about the *art* of leadership experimentation. The key is to *feel* leadership, just as Ted had imparted his wisdom onto me at the Surf Shack.

I struggled then and, to be honest, I still struggle.

When I exited the Navy, transactional leaders ruled the day. The Baby Boomer generation had a massive impact building the foundations of today's businesses and organizations from transactional-based thinking, doing, and decision making.

As leadership evolved, methods like Agile were introduced. Today there remains a power / leadership struggle. Transformational leaders are finding ways to *unravel* or *deconstruct* the decades-long transactional-based way of thinking and doing one technology, department, process, operational function at a time.

Today I struggle with what a lot of us are feeling: *there must be a better way forward*. Fortunately, there is a better way… that way being the evolution to becoming a *transcendent* leader.

Ken and I took a few months to settle on the term *transcendent leader*, which we are now bringing forward in this book. Why? To encourage conversation, experiential learning, and the creation of new *pathways* to becoming better, more thoughtful leaders. Pathways that evolve from the *constructive collisions* of our wisdom, the *experience and confidence to discern* (utilizing both traditional and energy-based information) and lead the way to help others think and do more *above the fray*.

Today I have evolved to where my leadership motto is *to lead from the heart with love, with a reverence for life*, as I help

> people and their organizations flow value to their customers.
>
> I hope that you too, will *struggle*, and reap the rewards of that struggle. Search for YOUR path and ascend as you move along your journey to becoming a thoughtful, transcendent leader, experiencing and feeling what we in our human language and form do not have words or ability to communicate … it can only be felt. —**JER**

The data, information, and knowledge provided in this book enables the reader to form insight and gain wisdom. We also hope it facilitates discernment. The result is the ability to navigate the path to becoming a more thoughtful leader. One who understands and is aware of how a manager evolves, how transactions can morph into transformations, and how mindset and intent can drive organization value beyond expectations.

Throughout this book we have introduced and referred to *the fray*. Below are some additional drivers or compounding sources which add to the frenzy, magnitude, and intensity of the fray. No other time in history has there been:

- as many different generations of workers in the workforce at the same time
- such a rate or speed of technology evolution and resulting disruption

- this magnitude of data disruption which comes from data combining with our advanced technologies
- political, ideology, and wars for power going on simultaneously
- mixing of government and technology by power brokers to achieve certain results

Adding to the leadership challenge is the fundamental shift in how organizations are run, being led, and managed. For a leader to lead successfully in this world, they have to be tuned in and responsive to the needs of the organization. In order to achieve results and succeed as a leader, they have to lead from *above the fray*. Of our three types of leadership, only transcendent leadership enables a leader to lead from above the fray.

Whether leveraging situational leadership opportunities with key followers, providing team building exercises, or modeling preferred behavior, the most enduring and resilient indicator as to whether or not an individual is an effective leader (regardless of type / style) is the extent to which they are perceived as such by members of the organization and other stakeholders.

Finally, a challenge for both the new and seasoned leader alike would be to ensure that change occurs when it is appropriate. Knowing there is something that needs to be done (transcendent) and understanding the meaning of why things must change is less effective if actual change (transformation) fails to occur.

This can be the biggest challenge of all since people typically gravitate to what they know and even if they can "change" and "try" it … the change may only be temporary.

Transact Transform Transcend

PARTING WORDS
Ken

Which leadership approach—transactional, transformational, or transcendent—applies to you? Perhaps none of them fit; if so, remember to discuss the gaps between these styles and your personality and values.

Of the three leadership types highlighted in this book, I'm more likely to be *transcendent*. To a small degree I'm *transactional*, especially when I'm acting in a role where I've been asked to help keep things as they are or to help stabilize an environment. My day-to-day type would likely be *transformational*.

Finally, leadership… really good leadership… takes time and perseverance to build. A thoughtful leader knows that they can't (or shouldn't) just *wing it* and not plan out their activities and the potential impacts of those activities on those around them.

A good leader is *authentic* and examines their actions on myriad levels. One of the best leaders is one who is more of a mentor—someone who really enjoys *passing along* life's lessons—an *authentic* leader, someone confident enough to be truly open and giving with advice. The uncomfortable leader is the one who *protects* and *hoards* what they know.

John

Vignette

Surround Yourself with Smarter Peeps

We were on a search and salvage operation with the Deep Submergence Unit (DSU) off the coast of Mexico. There was a high visibility aviation accident over the ocean, some witnesses saw the fireball from the shore, and people high above wanted answers.

We were stationed only hours away, which made us closest to do the search. We believed we were the best and this was our opportunity to prove it. The commercial companies thought they were the best, but we were closer. They were scrambling to get their assets on-site so for once, time was on our side.

Our job was to find the accident site and start searching for clues as to what had happened. We were several days into the scan of the ocean floor and pressure was coming from superiors. Those of us on site brainstormed how we could enhance our search. We wanted to speed up results, but we were running into challenges with topography and geography of the ocean floor.

We found and agreed on a solution and got to work. I asked

the Senior Chief what he thought of the situation. He took a long pause, measuring me up. Then he said, "Petty Officer Ruppel, I know we are going to succeed because I have surrounded myself with the smartest people I know who I believe can figure this $%@! out. I am going to sit back and let you guys do your thing, just don't #@*& it up."

With that, he leaned back in his chair, put his feet up on the console, and started chewing a new batch of sunflower seeds, spitting the shells into a cup. For the rest of the watch (about four hours) the Senior Chief gazed out over the sea, periodically checking in on what I was doing. A few weeks later, we found the accident site and began our search for answers.

Yes, we were the best at doing this type of search. We found the accident site a few days before the commercial teams arrived. Those extra days gave us some more time to do some detailed observations and seafloor mapping, setting up the salvage teams for success. —**JER**

*V*ignette

Letter of Encouragement to Younger Me

Dear John *(22-Year-Old Younger Self)*,

You have come such a long way in such a short time regarding your leadership qualities and skills. Saying that, here is some advice which I would like to pass along to you, so that we can enhance your / my development and provide some clarity or insight to the journey ahead.

To progress as a leader requires you to progress in your understanding and utilization of data. The progression from knowledge to gaining insight, to having wisdom, and ultimately the ability to discern takes time — a maturation process as one of your future mentors will say. This is why you feel frustrated. The social norms will use the words entitled, or entitlement, and confuse your belief and confidence in your leadership abilities with that of someone feeling they are entitled to lead. Be patient, do not let your emotions get the best of you. Take this time to understand what *wisdom* is and how to *discern*. Prepare and anticipate for the day to come when you will have the opportunity to demonstrate your leadership expertise.

To move to the level of a transcendent leader will require you to become one with yourself and those whom you serve and support for success. To become one will require you to become whole. To become whole will require you to feel worthy. To feel worthy, you will have to learn how to receive. I know these words may sound strange and have little to no meaning yet, but in time they will. To derive meaning from what I have just shared will require you to *FEEL your way*. By *FEEL* I mean what you feel at your core, the epicenter of your heart, as to the meaning and significance of these words. The strength and effectiveness of your leadership will come from your understanding and conviction of your belief in these words.

To best prepare you for the thoughtful journey ahead, I'd like to share this insight from the perspective of transparency (the *superpower of a transformational leader*), and the ability to discern, (the *superpower of a transcendent leader*)—one of your biggest challenges will be *culture* and *mindset*. Today's world is filled with ambiguity and chaos, driven in part by fractured messages, politics, ideology, and a general *noise* that make it difficult to operate as a transcendent leader. But I encourage you: *please don't despair!* The transcendent leader is guided by energy-based governance, not man-made governance. You will ascend and break through the threshold to rise above the fray and lead from *above the fray*. There will always be conflict, John—but *you* will be there too!

The best way I have found to break through the fray and lead above the fray is to focus on flowing value to the customer, not the politics, ideology, or tribalism. The best metrics I have found are the flow metrics associated with flowing value to the customer, and using what we at the Catalyst Team I call CANDID metrics.

The metrics for being a thoughtful leader are simple and can be summarized in one word: *CANDID*. CAN—*can* you put your head on the pillow when you go to sleep at night, can you rest knowing you have absolutely led in a direction that was best for all concerned, leading from love from your heart with a reverence for life (some relate to this as the golden rule). DID—*did* you have to apologize? Did you have to apologize for your behaviors / actions, what you said, how you made people feel?

A thoughtful leader thinks before saying or doing. If you find yourself apologizing, reflect and evolve your decision making so no apologies are necessary.

Reflecting back to when I was you, I remember seeing the world as black and white, binary, ones and zeros. However, this is not how the world truly works. You will be faced with several situations where your beliefs are going to be tested due to people having different perspectives. One of your big lessons learned is coming in about a year from now.

As parting words of wisdom or guidance, your strength has been and will continue to be how resolute and steadfast you will act and lead according to what you feel is right by your teammates and the customer. Yes, there are times ahead when you won't want to put yourself at risk, to take the path of least resistance. This is understandable, but I am here, I made it, and can say that you will be ok, you will make it through. Please realize the challenges of standing up for what is moral, ethical, and true will forge your leadership to be just, and people will trust that. From this trust, you will succeed where others have failed, and succeed in more ways than you can imagine.

Sincerely,

~ John *(Your Older Self)* —**JER**

This book is my three-decade journey in the making of my personal credo—that which makes me … me! How to succeed when failure is not an option. All throughout my career, and especially early on as I was in the Navy, I have been confronted with, and continue to be asked to create outcomes which do not currently exist or are said cannot exist.

People ask me why or how I can succeed with several others before me have failed. I am told I am extremely "open."

Early in my career, as I experimented, learned, and explored what it meant and how to leverage my being extremely open, I was led on the journey shared in this book, mastering the leadership skills at being transactional, transformational, and transcendent.

"You must find the place inside yourself where nothing is impossible." "In the process of letting go you will lose many things from the past, but you will find yourself. It will be a permanent Self, rooted in awareness and creativity. Once you have captured this, you have captured the world."
~ Deepak Chopra

To ascend to a transcendent leader, I had to ascend to operate and execute above the fray which required me to let go of my pride, ego, and what I thought was myself to truly understand who and what I am.

"You have been assigned this mountain so that you can show others it can be moved."
~ Mel Robbins

Today, I have awakened to realize that this journey is not about me, myself, my wants, or desires, but more about us as a whole… our connected-self connecting with others… all of us coming together as one, doing great things together for what is best for all concerned. Hence the ability to provide the leadership and empower the team to succeed and rally around the idea of flowing value to the customer.

Reflecting back to the surf shack with Ted eating breakfast burritos, I have added a third question to Ted's guidance. That question being "Can you and do you resolutely believe regardless … in yourself, in others, in miracles, that there are truths which we cannot explain or have empirical evidence, that there are things we experience in life which we cannot prove, understand, or describe, which are true, do exist, and are a part of our reality?"

The reason why this third question is so critical is that to truly ascend and be able to operate as a transcendent leader at a higher level of consciousness and intelligence, you will need to believe. There will be leadership moments requiring a decision where the energy-based universe around us cannot be explained or validated other than what we feel conflicts with what is happening or said.

Good luck on your endeavors and personal journey as you evolve to be the best transcendent leader you can be.

Please remember that Dr. Ken, the Intelligence Catalyst Team, and I are here to help. We would be honored to have the opportunity to serve and support you on your thoughtful leader journey.

SHARE YOUR STORY

Please visit our web site to *share your story* and become a member of our community for helping to improve leadership around the world.

https://leadtheflow.com/products-and-services/

Transact Transform Transcend

ACRONYMS

Learning models, especially mnemonics like the acronyms below (and presented throughout this book), help make complex ideas and processes easier to consume and, (more importantly) *remember*:

BOLD

A thoughtful leader must be BOLD:

B—Broad

Understands the business

Understands technology and how it impacts the business

O—Open

Motivating and creative

Leverages the power of communication

L—Loyal

Taps into the specific talent of the organization

Recognizes the value of differing perspectives

D—Deep

Is credible

Can walk the talk

CANDID

C
A
N

CAN you put your head on the pillow?
When you go to sleep at night, can you rest knowing you have absolutely led in a direction that was best for all concerned, leading from love from your heart with a reverence for life?

D
I
D

∞

DID you have to apologize?
Did you have to apologize for your behaviors / actions, what you said, how you made people feel?

DENT

This evolved from working with leaders struggling to come up with new ideas. *Making a DENT* encourages discovery, exploration, and *what if* scenarios — it became our rallying cry!

D—Disorient: Does the new idea cause you to think in a new way? Does it make you tilt your head and wonder... maybe?

E—Extend: Does the idea extend or move along another idea or thought? Does it add something... or does it revisit something already considered?

N—Navigate: Does the idea make it easier to understand something, see opportunity better, and help create a path to get to where you need to be?

T—Transform: Does the idea make you want to stop in your tracks and completely change direction?

INNOVATE

For helping *promote an environment of discovery and learning.*

I—Investigate: Explore and research new ideas or concepts.

N—Navigate: Possibilities, partnerships, and explore new environments for creativity and experimentation.

N—Network: Connect with others in your field to exchange knowledge and collaborate on innovative projects.

O—Originate: Embrace different perspectives and coalesce learning and findings into original work and new possibilities.

V—Vision: Develop a clear vision of the desired outcome or innovative solution.

A—Adapt: Be flexible and willing to adjust approaches as needed.

T—Test: Ensure innovations are repeatable, reproducible, and translatable while exploring, experiencing, and learning from both failures and successes.

E—Extend: Implement (not merely install) and integrate—put your innovative ideas into action.

LEAD

A thoughtful leader — at their core:

L — Listens — not just with their ears, but with their heart, their experiences, and with an *informed gut.*

E — Empathizes with their team — taking the time to lean in and share experiences, pay attention to the epidata swirling around everyone, and being aware of what is going on within the organization.

A — Absorbs and synthesizes activities and happenings all around.

D — Discerns, participates, and doesn't retreat — taking the time to comprehend and consider the whole environment and possibilities.

LISTEN

Listening is perhaps the most important tool for a thoughtful leader. A thoughtful leader listens authentically, taking time to absorb what is happening all around.

L — Learn

Try to learn as much as you can about as much as you can, from others, from the environment, from your team — learn from everything that's around you.

I — Interpret

*Take what you have learned and use it to interpret what
it means and represents for your organization, and for the
individuals on your team.*

S—Shape

*Everyone around you will tend to gravitate to what they
know; learn to help them shape what they know and bring
new ideas and new ways of thinking to the organization.*

T —Transform

*Be ready for transformation, not mere change (where
things may also change back or revert to the way things
were). Be ready to transform the organization and go a
new direction instead of just going the same old way.*

E—Evolve

*Evolution occurs when you're effective at all these things.
A thoughtful leader evolves.*

N—Nurture

*Take the time and the opportunity to nurture your team;
help them along, stay connected and engage them with
regular conversations. A thoughtful leader is always
ready to nurture next.*

APPENDIX

John and I had a bit more to share and we thought the Appendix would be a great spot to tell a few additional stories and reflect a bit on each. First, John's *Confidence to Lead*, which details his adventures in Scouting. Next is the graduation speech, *Extraordinary!* that I was invited to deliver to an amazing senior class of High School students in Wichita, Kansas a few years back. Finally, John takes us back into the deep with *Learning to Discern with Deep Sea Ops*.

Thank you for joining us on this heartfelt journey! —**KER**

Vignette

Confidence to Lead

As an adult Scoutmaster of a Boy Scout Troop, the Scoutmaster is the leader of the troop. Our troop's culture and mindset was that of boy- or scout-led, meaning the scouts lead as much of the operations of the troop as possible. Before taking on the role of Scoutmaster, I met with the troop's committee and provided an outline of the three-year transformation which would be required to further transform the troop's culture and mindset. To summarize, the Troop Committee was asking me to further enhance the scout's leadership of the troop. In order to accomplish the task, I would have to change the current transactional culture and mindset to be more transformational. In addition, both the scouts and adults would need to evolve.

Understanding the magnitude of change being asked, I went to the District and Council levels of the Boy Scouts of America (BSA) while the Committee went to the Troop's Sponsoring Organization with the three-year transformation plan. Everyone approved. Having this support was critical because over the years of the transformation, transactionally-minded adults did go to the sponsoring organization, district, and council to dispute the change and different approach… to keep the *current state* and not evolve into the transformational-based *future state*.

In year two (2) of the transformation, during our recruiting period, we had a family walk into the door. Mom, Dad, two sons and a daughter came in, looked around to see the layout of things, and slowly made their way to me at the back of the room. As the meeting was about to start, the Dad leaned over to me and asked me if I was going to go up front to start the meeting. I replied with a smile "no." Both the Mom and Dad exchanged looks of uncertainty, looked back at me, and then started surveying the room with much more scrutiny.

The Senior Patrol Leader with the Senior Patrol off to the side and the Patrol Leaders lined up in front, quieted down as the Senior Patrol Leader started our Troop meeting. The ritual of starting the troop meeting by saying the scout oath signaled our meeting was underway and the Senior Patrol Leader started the meeting's agenda. At that moment the Dad leaned over and asked if I was going to lead the meeting. I responded with a smile and said "I am." With that response, Mom and Dad shared a second round of looks that were a mix of uncertainty about their son's involvement with our troop and confusion about what was going on here!

A few minutes later, one of the Scouts in a Patrol started acting up. The Patrol Leader did their job, refocusing the Scout. A few minutes later the Scout acted up again. At this moment I leaned over to the parents and said, "Watch this." The Patrol Leader signaled for help to the Senior Patrol off to the side, and one of the Senior Patrol members walked over to the scout who was acting up, said a few words in his ear, and sat down beside the Scout for the remainder of the meeting while we were in meeting formation. While this was going on, the Senior Patrol Leader did not miss a beat, welcomed the prospect scouts and their families to our Troop and completed his part of the Troop meeting agenda. At that point I went up and led the adult portion of the troop meeting.

After the troop meeting, the visiting family approached me with a look of disbelief and amazement. I smiled warmly and asked, "Did you see a problem tonight?" The answer was, "No." I then asked, "Did you see a need for myself or another adult to intervene? Was there any chaos or a danger type situation throughout the meeting?" Again, the answer was, "No." For the next five minutes I described that what they had witnessed was the Scouts leading their peer scouts and the adults providing a leadership safety net and that our troop's culture and mindset is transformational-based. Our leadership communication, ethical and moral decision-making, and transformational leadership skills we teach our scouts in our scout-led model are skills which the scouts will not fully appreciate or realize until a decade from now, once they have had a few years as an adult in the workforce.

The same way I worked with the Scouts to be transformational leaders of the Troop is the same way I have and continue to mentor and train transformational leaders around the world... what we are providing to you, plus more, in this book.

Referencing the previous vignette, *Confidence to Lead*, the vision was for the Scouts to lead as much of the Troop's operations as possible. The challenge was many adults and traditional scouting programs had adult leaders in place with a ceiling of scout responsibility or leadership. The vision the committee, district, and council approved was to remove that ceiling, train the scouts on transformational leadership, and then have the scouts decide for themselves, through experimentation, just how much they wanted to lead. I had total belief in myself and the adults who understood the vision that our leadership was strong enough to endure and succeed. I had total belief in the scout's ability to lead, and once they gained some confidence, they would be able to lead the troop as a team of networked leaders.

Following the four core elements of transformational leadership, it took the first year for scouts, adult leaders, and parents to understand the vision. The scouts redefined and established their scout led operating model. Year two was about the scouts operationalizing the model. This was the hardest year because there was some really strong resistance. Year three was where we sustained and level set the model. Each year the senior patrol and patrol leader's grade came fifty percent on how well they led as a leader, and fifty percent on how well their successor led the following year. Instilling this culture and mindset of responsibility and accountability for their leadership and their successor's leadership was the mechanism which provided sustainability.

Was this always smooth? Nope ☺! We had moments of leadership crisis at both the scout and adult level. We had all sorts of leadership types, and the scouts from year to year had their own vision for the level of leadership they wanted to take on. The adults, being in a supportive or servant leader role was tough for many. This is where I had to create a leadership vacuum. I created a void of leadership by having the adult step aside and see how much leadership the scout would take on. Once the scout established their level of leadership responsibilities, the adult would work with the scout to be their safety net. The key for making it all work was vision. For three years, my visual was the troop's mind map where we worked out all the scout and adult positions. Without using vision and transformational leadership techniques, I don't believe we would have achieved the level of scout leadership we did.

As for the result, the troop's scout-led history was enriched. The Scoutmasters before me who set the foundation, enabled all of us to become what was considered the scout-led model to follow. I worked with other Scoutmasters in the district and council. As we had predicted about a decade later, and after the scouts had a few years under their belts in the workforce, they became the leaders and managers of key projects, initiatives—some of which were high visibility where failure is not an option.

Reflecting on this leadership experience with the troop, there was an underlying theme. The reason why I felt confident this troop could take on such a transformation was because of the scouts' appetite for leadership and the incredible job the adult leaders did putting in the foundation and creating the scout-led model. My purpose was to expand upon and evolve what currently existed. My confidence came from the simple fact that I believed with all my heart that the scouts and adults were capable and could lead through any challenges that might arise.

Vignette

Extraordinary!

I can remember sitting right where you are now, wondering what was ahead of me—something I suspect all of you are wondering today as well.

At the time, I really didn't think too much about what I'd accomplished while at school. I was too busy looking ahead.

It was only after I left, and had the opportunity for reflection, did I realize the value of what I learned and experienced in high school.

Compared to others of my age and circumstance, I was better prepared as a high school graduate. I was fortunate to have great teachers, mentors, and coaches, as well as innovative learning programs.

I sense the same about all of you today.

As I learn more and more about the Independent School, I suspect you probably feel just as I did: thankful … thankful for the experience and the opportunities to learn in such a great environment.

Of course, at graduation I, like you, wasn't really thinking about any of that at all. I was thinking of just getting away.

Getting past all of the tests, the exams, the finals. I wanted to get away and—just START!

My first message today is about that "spark". Those motivations you have right now, that "ready for ignition" feeling!

Ralph Waldo Emerson wrote:

"Nothing great was ever achieved without enthusiasm."

This particular quote is from one of Emerson's early essays (Circles) and he was also writing about the fortitude and courage necessary to "make a new road to new and better goals".

Enthusiasm is a key part of success and achieving great things, but Emerson was also trying to tell us that "much is possible and excellent that was not thought of".

Your experience here at the Independent School has transformed you. You are ready for the excellent things you'll do—that you have yet to think of! You are ready for a life that will, at once, frame you as a thinker, an inventor, and a lifelong learner.

In high school, I transformed from being merely a student to being a scholar. I developed a confidence that comes from being aware, being prepared, and knowing the purpose and value of humility... and grace.

I, like Emerson, want you to be on the lookout for new

opportunities to transform and to discover those "new roads and better goals" as you move through life.

Consider that much of what is possible and waiting for you out there has yet to be revealed!

Your high school experience has prepared you for the next part of your life; Emerson's reminder about being enthusiastic in our efforts is a good message to share with you as you graduate. You'll encounter things that will make you frustrated, uncomfortable, and even a bit scared. But you are prepared. You are ready! Be enthusiastic as you move on to accomplish the great things in your life that lie ahead!

Extraordinary!

I was on your campus a few weeks back, talking with several of you and getting to know more about the Independent School. I was struck by the conjunctive nature of everyone I met.

Here, you don't have to be this or that. You don't have to choose between this program or that program.

You can be involved in sports *and* drama *and* mock trials.

You are an "and" group, not an "or" group.

A lot like the sentiment expressed in the popular Dr. Pepper TV commercial from a few years back ... I believe it went something like low calories and great taste with an emphasis on the "and", as in you don't have to be either / or ... that you can, in fact, have more than a single choice.

You are an "and" group—not an "or" group.

Let's test that. Do you see yourself in the following? Are you an "and" person?

* You're a great student, AND always taking the extra step to do more analysis, to make a deeper observation
* You're a great friend, AND always available when someone really (really) needs you
* You're a great athlete / actor / scout / poet / volunteer AND always doing the extra things only true leaders do
* You have a great heart, AND are always willing to pay attention to the real needs of those around you, paying attention, listening authentically, and seeing some of the things others may miss

Being an "and" person tends to make you beyond normal. It makes you extraordinary—and being extraordinary yields extraordinary results!

Doing those extra things... looking out for the unusual, doing a bit more research, taking a few more calculated chances, attempting something new, being aware—these efforts will help you stand out and certainly make life far more interesting... and fun!

Finally, this makes me think of something the American author, Henry James, once said:

"Try to be one of the people on whom nothing is lost."

What a great quote! James was trying to convey that we should all endeavor to continue learning, continue to listen, continue to be relevant.

I first read that quote when I was 19—not much older than you all are now—and it really made an impact on me.

I've lived my life trying to become "one on whom nothing is lost". That is, trying to learn as much as I can, about as much as I can!

Whether learning to repair a car, leveraging a new technology, or grappling with the science of organizational change, I like to be aware of all that's going on around me. Whether knowing the types of birds visiting my backyard feeder, or simply what strange alchemy causes some summer tomatoes to thrive, while mine typically wither.

I've tried to lead a life of discovery. I encourage all of you to do the same.

I am proud and honored to celebrate this special occasion with you. I ask you to take your experiences and all you have learned at The Independent School with you as you go forward to make your mark on the world.

My graduation "gifts" for you are the three "E"s:

Enthusiasm for the new roads you'll travel on the way to the great things you'll accomplish!

Encouragement to think about how you might become "one on whom nothing is lost" ... always on the lookout for new opportunities and new discoveries!

Extraordinary results that require extraordinary effort— remember, doing normal things tends to yield normal results. *And who wants that?*

Congratulations graduates! Enjoy ALL that is ahead of you!
—**KER**

I remember the situation of this graduation address very well! The students, teachers, and the administration all operated with a unified focus—an orchestrated collaboration that ensured their success.

I'd visited the school many times, but at graduation the scene was like a Broadway show. Everyone was in place, confident of their role in the production, and ready to perform!

That my address was called *Extraordinary!* was very appropriate. I talked about being prepared for all that is ahead and ready for those *unexpected* and *unanticipated* moments—never had I experienced a more capable crowd ready to accept that message.

Vignette

Learning to Discern with Deep Sea Ops

On a blustery overcast afternoon while on the back of the DSVSS *Laney Chouest* (Deep Submergence Vehicle Support Ship) out in the middle of the Sea of Cortez, I was launching transponders to set up an array at the bottom of the ocean. This would serve as our underwater navigation system supporting live broadcasts of the Jason Project. Our live underwater scenes of hydro thermal vents broadcast all over the world would come from a manned DSV (Deep Submergence Vehicle) and an Unmanned ROV (Remote Operated Vehicle). A satellite dish on the ship maintained our satellite uplink.

One of the world's leading deep-sea navigators with over 5 decades of experience, my mentor and friend Tom, was next to me. Over the course of the upcoming months of this expedition, our ship would be host to the world's leading scientists of various disciplines, oceanic organizational leaders, military, government leaders and politicians from several countries. The *whole show*, as we called it, was dependent upon the navigation team, Tom and I, getting this underwater navigation system in place, operational, and accurate.

After deploying the first transponder, the second transponder on the ready, and having a few moments of quiet to think, I realized the magnitude of responsibility on me as our US Navy's Navigation Lead for this expedition. As I looked over at Tom, he was sitting on the deck, calm, relaxed but keeping an eye on the team and I to make sure we were doing everything right.

While we were getting ready to deploy the second transponder, Tom picked his head up, did a 360 survey of the ocean and sky above in all directions. Tom then radioed the bridge, asking them about wind and wave conditions. He then went into the control van anchored to the port side corner of the back deck and came out after a minute. "Change of plans boys, we are going to go to transponder position three, and come back to this one on our way back as we make the loop. Make sure we update our records on the details." By details, Tom meant frequency, tether length, and some other variables that we would need to update and later use during calibration / configuration of the navigation equipment and software.

With the transponders successfully deployed, most of the crew went to sleep. During the night Tom and I stayed up working with the first mate to ensure the underwater transponder net was correctly calibrated. We knew that to repeat dive accuracy and direct the vehicles to within a meter or two on the ocean floor in successive dives meant we had to get this right the first time; failure was not an option. The schedule allowed no time to run a second calibration pass when the first set of scientists and dignitaries were scheduled to arrive at 8am.

We sat there in the control van, watching the transponder sonar return travel times, doing manual calculations from time to time and making some notes, and keeping an eye on things. I asked Tom what transponder two was all about... why did we change the sequence? Tom looked at me for a moment and asked me if I had noticed anything at that time. Taking a moment to reflect, I said not really, maybe some wind shift. Tom stared at me for a moment and then for the next 20 minutes proceeded to walk me through what he had noticed, what was going on in his mind and inside of him at that moment in time.

What Tom had observed was that the first mate driving the ship had changed course a few degrees. Not a big change, only a few degrees of difference. Those few degrees could be the difference between a success and failure for deploying transponder number two.

I was shocked and stunned at the same time—from his attention to atmospheric and sea conditions, feeling the sea itself, changes in the ship's operations, people's attention to detail, his gut feelings, his intuition, and so much more. After he was done, there was a long silence as he gave me time to process. I responded with a reference based on my martial arts training from my Wing Chun Sifu including the use of Chi energy. For the remainder of the time calibrating the transponder net, about five hours, I was provided a deep dive opportunity regarding what Tom called "paying attention." In this book we would call it *awareness* combined with *the ability to discern*.

In the years to come, as I challenged myself to be the best leader I could be, it dawned on me that the lesson Tom truly taught me that day was much greater than awareness. The lesson was the use of awareness to feed critical data into having the ability to discern, which enables one to understand what is and how to be a transcendent leader. The hyper acuteness comes from the combination of using my physical and energy senses, experience, knowledge, wisdom, and so much more.

Since Tom's opening up to me, sharing his experience, I look at each leadership situation as an opportunity to learn more or share so I and others can better learn from one another. Together we can all evolve and be a better oneness and version of ourselves.

In case you are wondering, yes, the expedition was a success with over 50 live broadcasts to classrooms around the world. For some of the dives, students in their US classroom would pilot the ROV 5000 meters below the ship in the Sea of Cortez, on the ocean floor. For the final live broadcast, my wife and family watched on a big screen at SeaWorld Amphitheater in San Diego, a special production showing deep sea expeditions operating behind the scenes. As the show was signing off and zoomed in, I was able to wave and shout out "I'll see ya in a month," waving an arm of a teddy bear to the camera. —**JER**

During this era of deep-sea underwater explorations, there was a specific sequence of expedition processes we followed once on station. It helped to prepare the expedition area for deep sea operations using a variety of underwater deep-sea vehicles.

One of those events was the deployment of transponders which requires the ship to approach from a specific direction at a specific speed. We worked with the first mate driving the ship from the bridge to agree on the best way to navigate in accordance with what is going on with the weather and the surface of the ocean. In addition, we take into account what is going on below the surface in the water column. The intent of the transponder's trajectory of descent is to land the transponder's weight within meters of the target location on the bottom of the ocean. The navigation team is on the back deck of the ship launching the transponders.

As the ship approaches the drop point, a 20 to 30lb weight is dropped over the side. The weight is attached to a steel cable, a tether, which can range from 100 meters to as long as we need in order to have direct line of sight (or in this case line of sound) between the transponders so they can talk to one another. The transponders are connected to the other end of the tether and are buoyant—they float in the water column.

The precision of deployment is very critical to the success or failure of an expedition, especially when the bottom contours or topography aren't flat. Imagine having an underwater ridge between your transponders, or setting up a series of transponders on an underwater hillside or inactive volcano. The trick or challenge is to 1) have and maintain a direct line of sound between the vehicles who may be going up and down along these underwater ridges, 2) have a minimum of three transponders pinging to the underwater vehicles at all times, and 3) maintain constant pings to the ship on the surface of the ocean. I consider the creation of this 3-dimensional underwater navigational setup similar to playing a 3-dimensional chess game. It is all about the angles and options at any point in time.

On this particular expedition, we had a variance in ocean bottom contours of over 700 meters between transponder locations. This was a very high-profile expedition with live satellite shows spanning multiple countries. There was zero margin for error.

On this particular transponder deployment, we had a new first mate on the bridge with whom we had not worked before and was not experienced with transponder deployment operations. The subtle speed and course corrections made by the first mate using judgment, to provide the ship's occupants a smoother ride, conflicted with the transponder deployment plan. Tom reacted with his ability to discern what was happening resulting in a positive path forward for all.

This experience taught me the impact *a few degrees of change* can have on a situation and the *subtleness* of discernment. This experience taught me how *in tune with your environment* you must be, and the *level of awareness you need to operate* from within to be able to discern.

I am so thankful and grateful to the first mate and Tom. From this experience, I felt like I was finally able to understand what discerning means and how to use it.

Transact Transform Transcend

VIGNETTES

Following are the Vignettes presented within this book, JER is John, and KER is Ken:

ABOUT THE AUTHORS

Kenneth E. Russell, PhD

Photo Credit: New College Institute/K. Webster

Dr. Ken Russell is an award-winning technologist, trusted transcendent leader, and innovation amplifier. He is an author, speaker, and board member known for helping organizations define and pursue their transformation journeys with guiding experience, connections, conversations, and collaborations. Key to his success as an active practitioner and coach / mentor is helping senior executives embrace the value of values and prepare for next generation processes and workplace challenges (including resiliency, policy / process development, validation of technology vision / direction, road-mapping, and Enterprise Architecture).

Senior Roles / Projects / Investments include:

• Chief Information & Innovation Officer, New College Institute

- Human Capital Transformation Advisor, HSEC
- M&A and Private Equity Advisor / Practitioner— Organization, Technology, and Process
- Chief Innovation Officer, Curran Biotech
- VP of Digital Transformation and CIO, Pfeiffer University
- Chief Architect & Executive Director, Applied Technology Acceleration Institute
- EVP Digital Transformation & Emerging Markets, iTalent Digital Solutions
- Chief Information Officer, Murdock Research Institute
- Executive roles at Cisco, Bank of America, Duke Energy

A technology pioneer, Ken developed early Intranet systems for large banks which led to his participation in developing one of the first successful Internet-based training platforms.

John Ruppel

John Ruppel works with leaders, their teams, and their organizations around the globe to evolve *what* and *how* they interpret, understand, and discern—helping them realize successful results. John is often called in when others have attempted but failed to get a job done, a goal is thought to be impossible to achieve, an objective has never been done before, or simply when failure is not an option. Following are some of the organizations and agencies John has helped with global and industry leading initiatives:

- AWS
- Philips
- Cisco
- Buhler
- Pearson Publishing

- CA Technologies (Netegrity)
- CSC (Computer Science Corporation)
- NAVWAR (SPAWAR)
- DAU (Defense Acquisition University)
- US Navy

In this book, John shares his leadership evolution journey, and reveals in a pragmatic, straightforward manner what and how you can evolve to increase your success as a leader. The key is that a leader's growth is accomplished by self-realizing and self-actualizing, taking personal responsibility, and holding yourself accountable for your own growth.

John's career is a journey of continuous leadership improvement and growth, experimenting with leadership and leadership situations in an effort to be the best leader he can be and help others be the best leader they can be. Let us not forget to have some fun and enjoy the moment.

CITATIONS

Built to Last: Successful Habits of Visionary Companies. James C. Collins and Jerry I Porras. Harper Business, New York, 1994.

Examinations of leader effect behavior within successful Fortune 100 companies. Russell, Kenneth E. ProQuest LLC, Ann Arbor, 2006.

Leaders of ideas. Warren G. Bennis. *Executive Excellence,* *17*(2). 2000. pp.8-10.

Leaders: Strategies for Taking Charge. Warren G. Bennis and Burt Nanus. Harper Business, New York. 2007.

Learning some basic truisms about leadership. Warren G. Bennis. *National Forum, 71*(1) 1991. pp. 12-15

On Leadership. Gardner, J. The Free Press. New York. (1990). p. 35.

Primal leadership. Goleman, Daniel. Harvard Business Review, Boston. 2001. 79(11), pp. 42-51.

Project to Product: How to Survive and Thrive in the Age of Digital Disruption with the Flow Framework. Mik Kersten. IT Revolution Press, Portland, 2018.

Social Knowledge: Organizational Currencies in the New Knowledge Economy. Kenneth E. Russell, PhD, et al. Spencer House. San Jose. 2014.

Straight From the Gut. Jack Welch with John A. Bryne. Warner Brothers. New York. 2001. p.44

The Magic of Intuition Is Not Magic. Joe Dispenza. https://drjoedispenza.com/dr-joes-blog/the-magic-of-intuition-is-not-magic | 20 March 2017.

Toyota production system: beyond large-scale production. Taiichi Ohno and Norman Bodek. Productivity Press. Boca Raton, 1988.

What makes a leader? Goleman, Daniel. Harvard Business Review. Boston. 1998. 76(6), pp. 93-104.

www.ingramcontent.com/pod-product-compliance
Lightning Source LLC
Chambersburg PA
CBHW072352200326
41519CB00015B/3741